D0008223

FAITH AND REASON

ESSAYS IN THE
RELIGIOUS AND SCIENTIFIC IMAGINATION

FAITH AND REASON

ESSAYS IN THE
RELIGIOUS AND SCIENTIFIC IMAGINATION

by

FREDERICK PLOTKIN

THE KING'S COLLEGE LIBRARY
BRIARCLIFF MANOR. N.Y. 10510

PHILOSOPHICAL LIBRARY
NEW YORK

ACKNOWLEDGMENTS

Two of the following essays first published elsewhere are here reprinted with some changes, by kind permission of the original publishers. "Natural Fact and Poetic Insight" first appeared in *Hartford Studies in Literature,* I (1969), 71-82; "Augustinian Aesthetics Revisited," in *The American Benedictine Review,* II: 3 (1969), 342-351.

Copyright, 1970, by PHILOSOPHICAL LIBRARY, INC.

15 East 40th Street, New York, New York 10016

All rights reserved

Library of Congress Catalog Card No. 72-97937
SBN 8022-2322-2
MANUFACTURED IN THE UNITED STATES OF AMERICA

BL
56
.P55   108062

To the Memory of

BABA, ZAIDA, ROSE, FANNY, SAM, AND JACK

Table of Contents

FAITH AND REASON

ESSAYS IN THE
RELIGIOUS AND SCIENTIFIC IMAGINATION

Preface

We can understand something of what lies beyond our experience by considering analogous cases lying within our experience. Thus, the relations subsisting between the world and God, science and religion, man and history, and between God and the Godhead seem to be analogous, in some measure at least, to those that hold between the body (with its environment) and the psyche, and between the psyche and the spirit. In the light of what we know about the second—and what we know is not, unfortunately, very much—we may be able to form some not too hopelessly inadequate notions about the first.

To some, the simplicity of this argument may suggest that I have in mind some kind of hybrid or counterfeit philosophy which uses metaphors and poetic expressions when hard and rigorous analysis is required. Truly there is a way of speaking and writing on deep subjects which can appeal to undisciplined minds but to those who want truth is merely exasperating. It gains its effect by ambiguous words and by the use of emotional, instead of logical, associations. I am fully aware of this danger, and if in this preface I appear to suggest, for instance, that changes and interactions in the realms of nature, history and spirit can be described in terms of relativistic expressions, I invite the reader to wait for a proper explanation in the essays which follow.

The simple statement I wish to make here is that what we meet with in the world of religion has its analogies in history and art, and literature and science. Science deals with positive and negative energy and inertia; art with major and minor chords, the rise and fall of the accent and the limiting and controlling power on matter of the form. So ubiquitous, indeed, is the phenomenon of "relativity" in nature and art that it has found expression

11

even in religious philosophy, in all those systems which go by the
name of natural faiths.

The universality of these relations must not, however, be
exaggerated; for like most major philosophical attitudes, "relativity" can never find a complete or absolute expression, for
such attitudes not only carry ideational twilight zones but, as time
goes on, grow in their meaning and vary in the scope of their application. In the light of new experience and reflection they
need restatement. This is especially true of religion and religious
ideas. The philosophy of religion, more particularly, has an
ancient ancestry and older formulations, but its present vigorous
growth in a world that has more secular interests and more
scientific ideas than before demands new expression.

The essays that follow endeavor to state freshly some fundamental aspects of religion and religious faith in general; the aim
of each of these essays is not so much a rigid agreement or un-
animity of belief but rather a commonality of general attitudes.
The method relied upon in seeking an understanding of these
matters does not reject the empirical method of science above
allegedly superior methods; the world sought is nominally the
world of natural existence, since only this world can be naturally
authenticated. (These essays are also intensely concerned with
the aspirations of the human spirit—its love of freedom, its sense
of beauty, its hope of creating a better civilization. For the
attainment of these ends, a philosophy of religion that is at least
nominally empirical, that relies on intelligence, that finds the
good within actual existence without denying ideal possibilities
may render its fair contribution.)

Yet notwithstanding this *caveat*, a demurrer must be entered.
Natural science is empirical; but it does not confine itself to the
experience of human beings in their merely human and un-
modified condition. Why empirical theologians should feel themselves obliged to submit to this handicap, goodness only knows.
And of course, so long as they confine empirical experience within
these all too human traits, they are doomed to the perpetual stulti-
fication of their best efforts. From the material they have chosen to
consider, no mind, however brilliantly gifted, can infer more than a
set of possibilities or, at the very best, specious probabilities. The
self-validating certainty of direct awareness cannot in the very

nature of things be achieved except by those equipped with a moral astrolabe of God's mysteries. If one is not oneself a sage or saint, the best thing one can do, in the field of religion, is to study the works of those who were, and who, because they had modified their merely human mode of being, were capable of a more than merely human kind and amount of knowledge.

The world as it appears to common sense consists of an indefinite number of successive and presumably causally connected events, involving an indefinite number of separate, individual things, lives and thoughts, the whole constituting a presumably orderly cosmos. It is in order to describe, discuss and manage this common-sense universe that human languages have been developed. Yet whenever, for any reason, we wish to think of the world, not as it appears to common sense, but as a continuum, we find that our traditional syntax and vocabulary are quite inadequate. Mathematicians have therefore been compelled to invent radically new symbol-systems for this express purpose. But the divine ground of all existence is not merely a continuum, it is also out of time, and different, not merely in degree but in kind from the worlds to which traditional language and the languages of mathematics are adequate. Hence, in all expositions of problems of reason and faith in the philosophy of religion, the frequency of paradox, of verbal extravagance, sometimes even of seeming blasphemy. Nobody has yet invented a spiritual calculus, in terms of which we may talk coherently about the divine ground and of the world conceived as its manifestation. For the present, therefore, we must be patient with the linguistic eccentricities of those who are compelled to describe one order of existence in terms of a symbol-system, whose relevance is to the facts of another and quite different order.

"The study of religion"—in an age of secularism, empiricism, and specialization, such a phrase is bound to sound grandiose. Grandiose, perhaps, it is; but also a necessary corrective to much of the thought that prevails in society today. It reminds us that even when all the historical and sociological contexts of human experience have been explored, "the thing itself," the individual human being, will not be thereby grasped; and that even if science is taken in its broadest sense—as any explicitly methodical, discipline, rational endeavor—it does not exhaust the possibilities of human insight. It is in the context of this thought that the essays in this book seek to suggest that God may be worshipped and contemplated in any of his aspects. But to persist in worshipping only one aspect to the exclusion of all the rest is to run into grave spiritual peril. Thus, if we approach God with the preconceived idea that He is exclusively the personal, transcendental, all-powerful ruler of the world, we run the risk of becoming entangled in a religion of rites, propitiatory sacrifices and legalistic observances. Inevitably so; for if God is an unapproachable potentate out there, giving mysterious orders, this kind of religion is entirely appropriate to the human situation. The best that can be said for ritualistic legalism is that it may improve conduct. It does little, however, to alter character and nothing of itself to modify consciousness.

Things are a great deal better when the transcendent, omnipotent personal God is regarded also as a loving and benevolent Father. The sincere worship of such a God may change character as well as conduct, and may even do something to modify consciousness. But the complete transformation of consciousness, which is "enlightenment," "deliverance," or "salvation," comes only when God is thought of as immanent as well as transcendent, supra-personal as well as personal, and when religious practices are adapted to this conception.

The dangers today are quietism and antinomianism, a partial modification of consciousness in our secular world that is useless or even harmful, because it is not accompanied by the transformation of character which is the necessary prerequisite of a total, complete, and spiritually fruitful transformation of consciousness.

Finally, it is possible to think of God as an exclusively supra-personal being, and many of the essays which follow speak from this point-of-view. For many persons this conception is too "philosophical" to provide an adequate motive for doing anything practical about their beliefs. Hence, for them, it is of no value. It would be a mistake, of course, to suppose that people who worship one aspect of God to the exclusion of all the rest must inevitably run into the different kinds of trouble described above. If they are not too stubborn in their ready-made beliefs, if they submit with docility to what happens to them in the process of con-

templating, reflecting or worshipping, the God who is both immanent and transcendent, personal and more than personal, may
reveal Himself to them in his fullness. Nevertheless, the fact
remains that it is easier for us to reach our goal if we are not
handicapped by a set of erroneous or inadequate beliefs about
the right way to get there and the nature of what we are looking
for. To live, wrote Kafka in an aphorism, one must narrow
one's circle—but one must be certain that he has not hidden himself somewhere outside it.

I

Poetics of the Invisible

1. *The Myth of the Self*

The question, where Gnostic ideas come from, cannot be answered in a satisfactory way because the newly discovered documents have not yet all been published. But our evidence points in the direction of the astrology and magic of the Near East, and also of Jewish heterodoxy. Therefore the Dead Sea scrolls, the great discovery of our age, are of paramount importance also for the study of Gnosticism. The documents found in the neighborhood of Qumran reveal to us the existence of a pre-Christian and pre-Gnostic Jewish sect. It seems by no means excluded that the origin of Gnosis is to be sought not in Greece or Iran, but in Jewish heterodoxy. An awakening sense of mythology, which was a reaction to the austere and legalistic Jewish conception of monotheism, produced the first elements, or archetypal patterns, from which Gnosticism, blended with magical and astrological notions, took its course. So there is some hope that within a short time it may be possible to discern the Gnostic stream from its origin in Jewish heterodoxy towards its ending in Manichaeism. A new world religion comes to light.

The phenomenological school, more skeptical in its derivations and more respectful of facts, thinks it has a better conception of the historical evolution of Gnosticism than former generations had. But it also holds strongly that this religion has a sense in itself, which can be distinguished from other types of religion. Gnosis is always a knowledge of transcendent revelation, which makes the spiritual man aware of his real Self that is sleeping unconsciously in him, of its transcendent origin and ultimate destiny. This revelation has the form of a myth, not as a disguise of some

17

philosophical abstractions, but because the myth is the spontaneous and adequate self-expression of the Gnostic soul. Therefore this myth should be read as a poem of religious experience, a divine comedy of longing and grace, which interprets the Universe as a mirror of inner moods. Earth arises from the state of despair, water from the tears of sorrow, air from the solidification of fear, light from laughter; while fire, causing death and destruction, is inherent in all these elements, as ignorance lies at the root of the other passions. Gnosis is the myth of the Self. So the phenomenological school seems to offer a picture of Gnosis which from an historical point of view is less improbable than the ill-founded hypotheses of the *Religionsgeschichtliche Schule* and does justice to the inner sense of this religious movement. Gnosticism, as far as it was important for the history of mankind, started among the heretical circles, the Minim of palestinian Judaism; it is a myth strongly rooted in a certain psychological attitude, in which the relation of man to himself, the world, and God is expressed. How was this relationship conceived?

What was the relation of the Gnostic to this world, in which he had to work and live? The new documents show us in a striking manner how the Gnostic experienced this world as complete nonsense, a bad dream and a cheap illusion—the world is an illusion. This is stated by the author of the "Letter to Rheginos" in the following way: "When you read in the Gospel that Elias and Moses appeared on the occasion of the Transfiguration of Jesus on the mountain, you should not think that the resurrection is an illusion. Much more it should be said that the world—the cosmos—is an illusion: the living will die, the rich will become poor, everything changes, the world is an illusion."

This conception recalls Indian speculations about the world as a veil of Maya. But the comparison should not seduce us immediately into supposing that these ideas were borrowed from Indian sources. The historical links, which may or may not exist, do not explain how it could happen that men of the second century B.C. had such a gloomy conception of the universe. The Greek philosophers of the time still sang their hymns in praise of that precious jewel which was the cosmos. The second century B.C. was a happy, prosperous, peaceful era. And yet these men, these Gnostics, conceived the world as an illusion, not because they borrowed this idea from India, but because they experienced the world as such.

The Gospel of Truth contains a remarkable passage about the world as a bad dream. It is unique in ancient literature and can have been written only by a poetical genius, as Valentinus was. It describes the state of ignorance, inconsistent illusion and absurdity, to which man in this world is condemned. "Having no root, he thinks of himself: 'I am like the shadows and the phantoms of the night.' But when the light appears, he becomes aware that the fear which possessed him was nothing. So men were in ignorance of God, whom they did not see. When this ignorance created fear and trouble, made them uncertain, hesitating, divided and split, there were many vain illusions and empty and absurd fictions that vexed them, like dreamers in the grip of nightmares. You fly and do not know where, or you remain immovable when you are persecuting an unknown. You are fighting, give blows, receive blows. Or you fall from a height, or you fly in the air without wings. Sometimes it is as if you were killed by an invisible murderer, though you are not persecuted by anybody. Or it is as if you killed your neighbors, your hands are stained with blood. Till the moment that those who have gone through all these things, awake. Then they see nothing—those who have gone through all this—because these dreams were nothing. So they have thrown from them ignorance just as the dream that they also hold for nothing. And neither do they consider its works as realities, but they dismiss them as a nightmare."

Valentinus expresses here, what so many poets before and after him have stated, that life in ignorance is a dream. I think we may state that the Gnostic has no relation to the world. He is living in a possessed world and he knows it. Now, of course, this conception of the world sounds very strange to progressive people who know so much and are so perfectly convinced of progress and the power of reason. We may, however, ask, which approach to reality happens to catch the essence of being, the rational approach or the existential, which necessarily expresses itself in myth. The other day I re-read Dostoevsky's *The Possessed* where he describes the first beginnings of the movement which is now in power in Russia. He describes it as a contagious state of possession and demonic insanity. How different is this picture from that which Turgenev drew, with great sympathy for revolutionary youth, in his *Fathers and Sons*. But history has shown that Dostoevsky's outlook can be held with as good reasons as that of Turgenev. When the Dutch historian Huizinga reviews the situation of modern man in the modern world, he begins his work, "Shadows of Things to Come," with the words: "We live in a possessed world and we know it." This is pure mythology, and Huizinga knew it. But we cannot dismiss mythology when we want to express the essence of our being in the world. The rational approach to reality will always seem superficial and the existential approach fantastic. But both have their rights and it may be said that Valentinus, with the intuition of a poetic genius, expressed so long ago what our tortured generation considers as its last word: that man is confronted with nothing.

We now proceed to discuss the relation of the Gnostic to God. Living in the world, in his state of ignorance, the Gnostic does not know that there is a God. The God of the Gnostic is the unknown God, infinitely removed from this unhappy world and its bloody history, and so also from man. The unknown God is so completely transcendent that he cannot be predicated, not even as being. Some Gnostics daringly spoke about the non-being God, the nothing, beyond thinking and conscience and thought. And yet this unknown, this transcendent mystery, exercised a curious spell upon the Gnostic's mind. When God is absolutely unknown and unknowable, why should you speak about him? And yet the Gnostics were extremely eloquent when they had to express the idea in purely negative terms, that God is Depth and Silence. There was, according to them, an innate longing and craving in man to enter into a relation with this transcendent mystery. And those who had received the grace to speak about that unknown Source of all being, which contains the Universe and is not contained by it, spoke with joy unspeakable about this bliss unspeakable:

"Not only he is what is called without beginning and without end, because he is ungenerated and immortal, but as he is without beginning and without end, so in his manner of being he is also unseizable in his greatness, unfathomable in his wisdom, ununderstandable in his power, impenetrable in his sweetness. . . ."

"For, in fact, he is of such manner and immense greatness,

that nothing else was with him from the beginning, no place wherein he dwells or whence he comes or whither he returns, no archetype which he uses as an image for his work, no trouble which accompanies him in his action, no underlying matter when he creates the things which he creates, no substance within him from which he produces the things which he produces, so that he could be accused of ignorance."

"But as to himself, as he is and as he existeth and according to his manner of being, it is not possible that the intelligence knows him, nor that a word is capable of expressing him, nor that he can be seen or traced, owing to his unfathomable greatness and incomprehensible depth and immeasurable height and his unseizable will. . . ."

"He is unknowable, that is, unthinkable by any thought, invisible in any way, unspeakable by any word, untouchable by any hand: he is the only one to know himself."

These quotations, taken from the Treatise on the Three Natures, show convincingly what the Gnostics meant when they spoke about the unknown God. God is infinitely far above; man is on the earth, where he does not belong, a prey to possession and in complete ignorance of his transcendent origin and destination.

This complete lack of relationship is restored by the revelation of the Gnosis, mediated by the Savior, who is Christ.

The Gospel of Truth contains a wonderful passage about the appeal to man by Christ, which makes him aware of his transcendent origin and ultimate destiny. Man, it seems, is conceived as a mountaineer who has lost his way and is wandering in the fog. Then he hears his name called; he knows where he came from and where he has to go to find his way back. The passage is perhaps the most characteristic of Gnosticism and clearly shows that Valentinus was both a poetic and a religious genius.

The Living Ones—that is to say, the Gnostics, whose names have been written in the Book of Life—receive their instruction for themselves alone. They turn to God in whom is the perfection of All, because they are those of whom the Father has known the names from the beginning and who are called at the end as beings who know that it is they whose names the Father has called. "Therefore he who knows is a being from above. When he is called, he hears, he answers, he turns himself towards him who calls him.

He comes to him, he understands how he has been called. Having the Gnosis, he fulfils the will of him that has called him and wants to do what pleases him. He receives rest. He who thus has the Gnosis, knows whence he came and whither he goes; he understands as a man who has been drunk and awakens from the drunkenness wherein he was and comes to himself." The Word of Christ is an event, an appeal which uncovers our deepest and innermost being; reminds it of its noble origin and glorious destiny, delivers it from the nightmares which it has produced by its unconsciousness and makes it aware of its unworldly essence. So through the appeal of the Savior, which finds an echo in the spiritual man, the relation to God has been restored, and also relation with the True Self, that divine spark of spirit which dreams unconsciously in man. Christ, for Valentinus, is the Word of God, which reveals man to himself.

It is this discovery of the unconscious Self which really matters in Gnosis. The whole religion can be summed up in the words of a Valentinian: "The spirit, having become conscious of its origin, returned to its origin." The complicated systems of Valentinus and Basilides in the second century, of Mani in the third century, are rooted in this basic experience. And the Gospel of Truth shows that this experience can be expressed even without a complicated system, which is still absent from this early writing. I think the new discovery plainly confirms the conception that the Gnostic myth is a projection, or, perhaps better, an expression of an emotional and overwhelming, irrational religious experience, the experience of the Self.

Thus man has gained, through revelation, a relation to himself and so to the unknown God. But what is the relation to his neighbor? What are the ethical implications of this religion? It is a very striking feature that in the Gospel of Truth ethical teaching is completely lacking. No commandments, no ethical considerations, nothing. Of course, it is very possible that Valentinus was a decent man, who behaved according to the rules of Christian or pagan morals. But Gnosis as such does not have ethical implications. It even seems that as often as not the Gnostics despised a proper behavior according to the teaching of the Bible. They divided mankind into three classes which were different by nature: (1) the materialists, who were very bad and would perish without exception; (2) the psychics, the ordinary churchgoers, who had to do good works to be in their way; and (3) the spirited men who will be safe in any event, saved by nature, as they say. And, of course the Gnostics belonged to those happy few who delighted in esoteric knowledge about the higher worlds and were too exalted to care about social obligations and social duties. Sometimes they taught a double morality; one for the mob, which is identical with the teaching of the church; and one for the Gnostics, which dismissed all categorical imperatives and looked on the world and the neighbor merely as means of self-realization.

In view of this, it is time to recall the distinction made by the Fathers of the Church, as well as by the apostles, between falsely so-called Gnosis and true Gnosis. Of course, these Fathers had perfectly good reason for rejecting the heretical Gnosis of their time; but at the same time they tried, with some success, to integrate the precious moments of this Gnosis into their own conception of Christianity. Clement of Alexandria and Origen claimed against Valentinus that they were the true Gnostics. Perhaps the theological disputes of that time are no longer relevant to modern man. But the problem as such still exists and can be put in modern terms. The false Gnosis does not know the encounter with another person. It considers man as an atom without windows, which must develop itself at all costs. Imagine those old gentlemen, those dear ladies, who are so entirely concentrated on their divine self. Even intercourse with women becomes a means of self-realization: it enables man to experience his transcendent, hermaphroditic unity. As a matter of fact this was what the Valentinians of the second century taught. Then, however, man does not meet another being, whose other-ness he respects, but uses his neighbor as an instrument. That is the false Gnosis. To the Gnostics of this kind, the apostle Paul says: "If somebody imagines that he has Gnosis, he has not yet learned to know as he ought to know."

When then is true Gnosis? From the Christian point of view, true Gnosis considers the encounter with the neighbor as a religious experience. There exists a saying of Jesus, not contained in the Gospels, which nevertheless may be authentic: "Have you seen your brother, you have seen your Lord." The neighbor is a mysterious other, who comes on our way and represents the Lord. The poor, the miserable, the sick, the doomed should be seen,

really seen, because behind them, in solidarity with them, is the
Suffering Servant.

Of course, the Gnostics were and are right in their criticism
of current Christian morals. The Christian faith, however, is not
a credulous acceptance of what the Church says or the Bible says,
but is the personal encounter with Christ. Those who have some
insight into the person of Jesus affirm that this encounter must
have, and cannot but have, ethical implications. The consequence
of this encounter might be that man becomes one with the mob,
the condemned, or even humiliates himself so far as to range
himself among ordinary churchgoers.

And this encounter will certainly change his attitude towards
the world and its suffering. For Paul, the Gnosis of Christ
implied the voluntary acceptance of world suffering: "If we know
Christ and the communion with his suffering and the force of his
resurrection." The false Gnostic rejects martyrdom; Origen died in
consequence of the wounds inflicted on him during persecutions
by the State. Now imagine a spiritual leader who tried to persuade
his fellow-religionists not to resist the totalitarian State. Would
not he be, for all his spiritual insight, a false Gnostic? So we may
imagine that the Christian Church, even of our time, would
reject a Gnosis which considers man as a spiritual atom without
windows, a self-realizing individual lacking relationship with his
neighbors. But the judgment of the Fathers was not only negative.
Some of them knew perfectly well how unspiritual the mass of
Christians can be, and how unsatisfactory for the religious tem-
perament the answers of the official Church sometimes are.
That is why they presented their teaching as the true Gnosis.
For Gnosis it remained. And it is most appealing for a modern
mind to see how practically all the Fathers of the Church, not
only Origen but also St. Augustine, speak about the Gnosis of the
self. They have integrated this conception in the whole of their
teaching. According to them, knowledge of your self is a stage on
the way to knowledge of God!

Were they right? Is it Christian to speak about love for your
self, as for instance St. Augustine does? The great commandment,
the corollary of the Christian religion, is to love God and your
neighbors as yourself. This, it seems, does imply that man loves
himself. It is shown to him how he will be a proper man, an *imago*

Dei, when he answers to the Calling of Christ, the Word of God, and so encounters his neighbor. Then he really is himself in his relationship to the other. Then he really loves himself. Therefore, I think, the Fathers of the Church were quite right when they considered the Gnosis of the Self as part of the Christian religion. It is perhaps a merit of the heretical Gnostics that they drew the attention of their contemporaries to this unconscious Self that is sleeping in man.

2. *Adam's Vision*

If, for the purposes of analysis, we restrict our interest in the first three books of Genesis to dynamic and simple components of large complexes of ideas, we discover that any former perspective we may have had with regard to ideas in the text soon evaporates. We tend to lose interest in the properties of ideas themselves and tend to become interested more in the properties of the relationships between ideas. We come to view the text as possessing certain inexpungable traits of pluralism.

Our "total" experience of the text, viewed formerly as a temporal phenomenon, i.e. as a direct, discontinuous experience of knowing something which is inappropriate to recurrent types of phenomena, is no longer as important to us as apprehending the intentional character of our experience of knowing. In other words, we tend to become metaphysicians.

The theory of knowledge we are led to develop tends to be dualistic in the following way. Once we legitimize our isolating for consideration only one property of the glue which holds two specific ideas together—because it is *this* property, and not others, which we presume to be the reason why it stands in the relationship which it does to the specific ideas with which we are concerned—our experience of the text is fractionalized. In a special way, ideas become representative for us of their function. In short, knowing and experiencing cease to be the same.

It may be argued, of course, that a phenomenological approach to the forms of knowledge and experience relevant to Genesis is limited because there are elements in biblical epistemology, for example, which analysis cannot completely account for; we respond by noting that any canon of evidence at our disposal—theologically convenient or easily visualized— demonstrates that knowledge of facts and knowledge of judgments of effects are both a part of the same complex, and that the total view should include both.

One point in our preliminaries remains unclear however. At the onset of the reader's phenomenological vision, the text of Genesis seems equidistant from three primary mountains, the world, man, and God. It is difficult indeed to discover a method which insures the reader a clear, uninterrupted view of the peaks, since they are so often covered with clouds. In addition, owing both to the nature of the reader's location and to the fact that the peaks in question cannot be clearly seen at the same time, experi- mental verification of their presumed nature is prevented.

Is there anything true (in the primary, not the ultimate, sense), we are led to ask, or anything which aspires to *become* true in the statement that a reader destroys any possibility of achieving knowledge of the text and his method of acquiring knowledge unless he begins with the commonplace that the "knowable" in the text is something rather than nothing, some- thing—not I, not God, not everything? Apart from its initiatory function, it is clear that the statement turns out to be as inadequate and misleading as the question which brought it into existence.

Preliminary knowledge of the first chapter of Genesis pre- supposes that the world is something. Indeed, when we look closely, we notice that the world retains an element of variability. For some men, the name "world" exists through general consent; not so for Genesis, which also decides, within limits, what its character has been in the past, and shall be, in the future. The word indicating the thing, then, is not the thing itself, and the classification is not the character or action which it classifies. The designation chosen by Genesis is clearly the only immutable factor.

In the context, the "world"—and, by extension, man, and God —clings to this designated something in a purely external manner. The world can suffer a curse upon its ground, it can support four rivers, designated by names, and so on.

The reason why the text indicates the existence of something beyond the world while saying that the world is something now becomes clear. The companion of everything, yet external to everything is language. If the world is truly something permitting the existence of other things external to itself, language must be a normalizing and projecting bridge between the world and those things external to it. And that is precisely what it is.

"Language" is a simple word. It neither can, nor wants to be, the essence of the world. Even though it appears to function in a deeper region, it merely names the things of the world. When Adam assigns names which find their ways to things, he is uttering words which witness his existence. When he speaks, he is sacramentalizing his being by affixing his seal to this external reality. Adam's word is not a part of his world; it is his seal.

To say that a mere name of a thing is external to it is also simple. This "merely," however, implies that it might have a different name. Applied to Adam's *own* proper name, this might appear quite absurd. After all, under ordinary circumstances when a name is required, the one who is named is driven into the presence of his own mind, to the internal by which he is dominated in order not to take refuge in the laws of the past which always act from without but to divest himself of the external. Hearing his name spoken, the one named recognizes himself and knows that he is present. In this sense, a word may both represent and validate the continuity of existence.

True enough that Adam, hearing his name spoken, knows himself as present; but what, we may ask, constitutes Adam's knowledge of his own existence and the existence of his external world, Eden? How does Adam learn of Adam and of Eden? Since the transcendent entity which Eden represents, because of its nature, is a characteristic of Adam's objective world, Adam can probably have real knowledge of the relationship between his ideas which represent immanent objects of knowledge and ideas of transcendent entities. The reality of his modal ideas of Eden is not dependent upon the existence of the external reality of Eden; since mythical realities may be constructed without reference to objective archetypes, their reality is not contingent upon such a correspondence.

Of the two primary elements of knowledge by which Adam can establish certainty or uncertainty, judgments of probability with regard to real knowledge are clearly impossible. Adam has no past, nor any memory of a former existence, and probable epistemological judgments clearly depend on the remembrance and recovery of former intuitions of objective reality. Adam, then, is restricted to using judgments which incorporate intellectual rectitude as well as perceptual certainty. He identifies that form of cognitive thought which yields objective certainty with knowledge; and, to the extent that he links knowledge to a particular perception which apprehends relationships and repugnancies of, and between, objective and transcendent ideas, Adam is a Lockean.

To clarify further the issue, an examination of Adam's statements on this subject is in order. On three different occasions, Adam remarks:

> And Adam said, This is now bone of my bones, and flesh of my flesh: she shall be called Woman, because she was taken out of man. (2:3)
> And he said, I heard thy voice in the garden, and I was afraid, because I was naked; and I hid myself. (2:10)
> And Adam called his wife's name Eve; because she was the mother of all living. (2:20)

From these utterances, it follows that certainty constituted by knowledge is achieved by some faculty of perception which involves an ability to apprehend the signification of signs, and an ability to perceive the ideas themselves as objects. When perceptual conditions of certainty such as "hearing" God's voice or "beholding" the Woman are not realized, uncertainty is always present.

If Genesis is suggesting that certain innate principles of perception are pre-conditions for knowledge and experience, which may also require external stimulation in order to become accessible to introspection, this would in effect, link the question of human knowledge to rationalistic psychology. Even more, this would lead to the hypothesis that the organization of phenomenological data in terms of relationships, function, judgments, and gestalt qualities is the result of a perceptual power which provides any object of thought with a suitable occasion to exercise and make manifest its intelligibility from within itself in an extremely subjective manner.

Though Adam's reliance upon the claims of intuitive knowledge is rather slight—he does not, we notice, perceive the self-evident in nature as irresistibly and as consistently as he would like—his effective dependence upon demonstrative knowledge is far less productive. Demonstration (dependence upon evidence not perceived directly) has, for Adam, far more subjective obstacles than intuition, since it depends on memories of previous intuitions about the subject-matter (of which Adam has none) and, of course, the subject-matter itself.

The definition of knowledge employed by Adam, then, commits those who operate within its area of dominance to an intentional sort of extreme subjectivism. One implication of this definition is that the function of an idea, related as it is to its locus, is also involved in the very nature of the idea itself, and because of that, is a cornerstone of the activity of perceiving relationships between ideas.

External relationships between ideas as objects and ideas as signs which represent reality, in this sense, point to the significance of the intrinsic nature of the ideas. Perceptions of these relationships, then, are dependent functions of the objects of Adam's thought. This means that the objects and the relationships in an absolute sense, namely, the world (Eden) and God, must finally be determined by the objects and their loci. Because of this, perception of this variety of knowledge involves the knower in the objective necessities of apriorism. Indeed, this should hold regardless of whether the objects of thought are mythically objectified or not.

Apriorism is not so successful a method when used by Adam to verify the claims to reality of substance, however. Faced with the clear fact of Eve's existence, Adam remarks: "she shall be called Woman because she was taken out of Man." One would imagine that at the very least Adam would assert that if ideas of substances derived from experience on ontological grounds, then knowledge of the reality of these substances would be possible for him. Instead, he offers us a quantitative comparison of the substance in question which asserts the scope and character of its existence cautiously and with probity. It is as if he is aware that a probable or possible existence attributed to a quality of an object is enough

to prevent the reality of that idea of substance from being substantiated to any degree of certainty. In other words, this kind of
probability cannot be determined on a priori grounds.

In this regard, the manner in which Adam draws quantitative
distinctions is of considerable interest. When Adam describes Eve
in terms of flesh and bone, he is stating an analytic proposition
whose predicates signify one element of an idea for which its
subject stands. The epistemological function of this proposition
is clearly limited, and Adam knows it, for his analytic judgment
can neither extend his knowledge nor distend his soul; its "certainty" vis à vis Knowledge is restricted to the merely verbal
level. Adam is aware, on the other hand, that for positive knowledge, a perception of the relationship between ideas is required,
regardless of whether the propositions are real or probable; that
is, a perception that extends beyond analytic, or what may be
termed, synecdochal propositions.

In terms of the fixed spatial, and temporal structure of human
consciousness and the demands of the process of human experience,
how can this representation of the function and constitutive process
of human knowledge in Genesis be justified? Only one explanation
seems likely. Were it possible to analyze the character of human
experience and human consciousness in a thoroughly deductive
manner, then all empirical and anthropological apriorism would
be expunged. Moreover, this reply would in no way be consistent
with the position expressed in the Sapiential books to the effect,
owing to the interpenetration of the world of spirit with the world
of nature and of transcendental law with the historical process, the
intentionality of human existence is ultimately relative; or, expressed in theological terms, theological determinism—since it
is contingent upon more than the transcendent in nature—is a
provisional and partial fact of nature. In this context, salvation is
related to the working out of particular covenant obligations
between God and man which link, but do not fix, in a rigid way
the relationship of the real temporal order of the actual world to
the supratemporal.

The significance of this belief in the intentionality of existence
is clear when we return to our discussion concerning Adam's
name. Earlier, it was suggested that Adam's name being spoken
provides him with the opportunity to discover himself as present.

This would be to assert that his name—which signifies his permanent existence in an internal, conscious sense—accomplishes what he himself cannot: to endow him with authority over time, which, if accomplished, would result in a permanent condition of Adam being present to himself.

If this were possible, Adam's reason would suffer irreparable damage. Discovering himself from instant to instant, Adam would vanish from instant to instant, eternally annihilated by the temporal claims of cause and effect. Neither the possibility of covenant liberty nor the occasion for Reason to operate as choice exist for Adam, therefore. If a moment exists when Adam can be free, it is already gone. His Fall, or, more accurately, his falling, is constituted, then, by his involuntary loss of his presence in the present which is caused by his efforts to transcend both the transcendental laws of cause and effect governing his being and the temporal laws of the historical process.

It is not surprising that the repetitive process which causes each moment to be reborn continually resembles, to the degree that it does, the course of Adam's future life after his creation. It is Adam's future life, after all, from which the opportunities for him to perceive his own existence immanently are drawn.

Because the make-up of his consciousness is such that Adam is summoned to live his unique existence, and, at the same time, speak, hear, and behold, Adam's future is guaranteed; he must live despite the fact of numerous "falls." His name, the very word "Adam," however, neither coerces nor liberates him. Because it is mere word, and hence, merely an object of thought, it signifies a particular something beyond Adam himself and points to a final conformation with an ideal. That ideal, and its locus vis à vis the object of Adam's thought are particularly important, and to that we now turn our attention.

First, we must establish whether or not knowledge of the transcendent is possible in Adam's consciousness. If we examine Adam's remarks about his creation, we discover that his utterances are characterized at first by no assumptions of any kind about existence; he restricts himself to his own conscious experiences. In order to move from this nearly solipsistic stage of pure consciousness, Adam next attempts to establish the reality of "others" like himself but since his uniqueness is not yet clear to him, Adam may be allowed to confuse momentarily his own pure consciousness with what he mistakenly regards as the ego of the natural world.

It was noted earlier that Adam's name cannot liberate him; on the other hand, the method used to enclose Adam in an idealized subjective structure cannot fail to function as a liberating influence on his thinking. In the sense that whatever ol 'ect perceived by Adam is considered valid and certain, he is liberated from the claims of presupposition and belief. All objects of knowledge become correlative functions of his experience.

The question raised earlier may now be placed in sharper perspective. If Adam is operating within the idealized structure of his inner world of consciousness, and if, as it has been suggested, the route his experience will take is contingent in some way upon the transcendent world of existence, how must our claims concerning the mechanics of Adam's subjective consciousness be altered? Should they be altered at all?

First, it is necessary to recall that the method employed by Adam's conscious mind to define both a distinctive area of inquiry and a special object of inquiry is neither hampered by, nor dependent upon, psychological requirements. Since clarity and certainty are Adam's goals, Adam is faced with an apparently insurmountable problem if he imagines that he can know the unknowable and experience the experience beyond itself. If a priori transcendence or transcendent knowledge were really possible for him, he somehow would have to possess the ability to perceive directly and totally the relationship of knowledge to its transcendent object, of say, man's mind to God. This he clearly cannot do.

Adam is compelled, then, to delimit the transcendent world of existence in order to bring it to self-givenness. In other words, when he reduces his knowledge of the transcendent to the area of pure, subjective consciousness, he is eliminating transcendence from his experience. This reduction, of course, is undertaken only after his efforts to rise beyond the transcendental laws of cause and effect have failed. But when it is accomplished finally, Adam has irremediably fallen.

That he must fall from the transcendent reality of existence, given the make-up of his conscious world and his epistemology, is clear when we recognize that the transcendent cannot be reduced to immanent perception the way the immanent can. By nature, its existence must be uncertain and problematical. This is why the Creator appears to Adam under conditions which we may term artificial—in a dream vision. If the transcendent is reduced to a dream object, it no longer becomes objectionable as a possible false abstraction, a danger which Genesis would indubitably have risked if it had transformed the Creator into something capable of being experienced—with a visual content, with a body of apperceptions, and so on. But what becomes of our argument when Adam's dream is transformed into an immanent one?

First, we are not confronted with a riddle when Adam sees his Creator. Though the transcendent preceded all perception, perception is nevertheless a constituent of the experience of transcendence. Evidence of perception, in addition, has an immaterial quality; since evidence must be a function of the existence of the necessary object of perception, evidence contains elements far more complex than simple immateriality. In short, things correspond to the perception, whether or not the thing is immanent or transcendent. The transcendental world of existence exists and may be perceived; this claim does not do away with our argument. The potential epistemological dilemma is removed when we remember that the dilemma results from the fact that Adam's aggregate experience is sealed, isolated, and set off from the external reality of everyday life. It is not unusual, in other words, to find the transcendent inhabiting a mythological environment.

Second, it may be deduced from God's appearance that Adam needs to see God and that God is under an obligation to make himself seen. This becomes clear as soon as we recognize the special conditions that obtain when the creator of the name actually confronts the thing named. When God still exists only as a dream object for Adam, his name "Adam," is merely a cognomen. Of course, at this point Adam has other names which he has not received; he already possesses them. As soon as his names are uttered, they adhere to him. The name "Adam," is also the word of God. This implies the certainty that God's presence is implied by it, not merely a probability. The Creator's word implies the presence of the Creator and that someone to whom the word is spoken—and so also with the word of Adam. When God is absent, that is, when Adam dreams, the word of God does not force itself upon Adam's consciousness. The existential reality

of the Creator's language, then, stamps the sign of God upon
his creature. Though Adam is not an illusion when asleep, he
certainly cannot gain in definition by being isolated from an external perceivable reality.

Third, experience and knowledge in Eden are always "of"
something. A priori knowledge of pure phenomena, however,
cannot be denaturalized, *viz.,* disengaged from its antecedent
naturalistic environment. Only when one ignores the character of
Adam's natural setting in Eden does the epistemological riddle
implicit in Adam's perception of his Creator become possible;
possible, though still unwarranted. Though Adam asks, in the
course of his "awakening," for evidence of other egos and the
existing world, he is certainly obliged to his external reality for
providing him with the occasion for reflection and inquiry.

The only effective argument against Adam's true perception
of his Creator consists in claiming that his Creator is transcendent in a non-psychical sense—and that, of course, is absurd. That
is not to say that when Adam perceives his Creator, he is in the
presence of transcendental certainty. There is room enough in
Genesis for formalism, or fantasy, for that matter; but there is
also an end to both. If we deny that Adam "sees" the transcendent,
we are hardly better off than he is. Can we ever say about our subjective world that we are certain that it *is* while it is, but not quite
so sure that it *was?*

In order to reconstruct the mechanics of Adam's "knowing"
the Godhead, it is necessary to discover the correlations between
Adam's external world and his conscious, inner world. When Adam
says "I heard thy voice," that statement has two meanings: first, as
an intentional correlate of Adam's existence (his existence is
immanent, absolute, and logically conceived); and second, as an
assertion of ego-presence in the sense that his existence is confirmed to be in accord with his own consciousness.

From Adam's point of view, the transcendent being of
Adam's Creator is never complete. For him, the Godhead
initially is an object of relative composition, relative shape,
relative certainty, and even relative divinity. His Creator's being
is almost accidental. It is possible to say, however, that when
Adam focuses his consciousness upon his Creator, the partial in his
natural experience (Eden) is transformed into a whole in his

inner, subjective experience. By means of this procedure, Adam acquires a special existential context which provides a *place* towards which the transcendent can move, be received, and most important of all, a place which constitutes it and gives it form, presenting it with human values and framing it in human terms.

With consciousness providing his natural point-of-view, Adam directs his thought upon his experiences in Eden and apprehends them as existence. If Genesis has Adam perceive God through the artificially detached experiences of dream vision, it is isolating Adam's knowing self in order to demonstrate the impossibility of three things: isolated self, experience without causality, and life without the transcendent which constitutes life. As long as no metaphysics is introduced into Adam's internal world, Adam is free to pursue his inquiry into the structure of knowledge vis à vis God, the world, and himself.

For Genesis, God is not to be found at the conclusion of a syllogism, nor is his being inferred from historical or psychological evidence. Adam has no history; neither does his perception. Though unseekable and undemonstrable, God can nevertheless be reached by experiencing the nothingness of self. If Adam renounces universals, causality, necessity, and empiricism, then he can be free. But in the face of the natural necessities of Eden, Adam cannot refuse to reject *veritates aeternae*—what we term the self-evident today—as anything but illusions. He cannot confront his existence directly, and so, cannot experience authentic freedom from the constraints of the laws of natural necessity.

According to Genesis, knowledge leads to death. It is this mere commonplace which hurls us into the realm of the purely arbitrary, into a region where it is impossible for thought to orient itself and where it cannot lean on anything. If the view of human reason held by Genesis is correct, even if knowledge, by introducing itself into being, leads to indubitable existence and to death—then Adam can never cast off reason or disavow choice. He would be imprisoned by truth itself, and be forced to withdraw into an ideal world of his own making.

But knowledge does not justify being for God; rather, it is from being that knowledge achieves its justification. In other words, it is Adam's mind that chokes the tree of life, not the tree of knowledge.

The "given" does not dominate Adam; it determines neither his present nor his future. In Eden, knowledge is radically wrenched away from existence and becomes, in Luther's language, *bellua qua non occisa homo non potest vivere* (the monster without whose killing man cannot live). Because the data of experience coming from the merely immanent reality of Eden constitutes a kind of autonomous knowledge and an autonomous ethics, all that is discoverable as material and ideal leads Adam to the plane of the petrified "it is," that is, away from truth.

An ethic plundered by, and from, the senses, therefore, can never unmask, for Adam, the truths that enter into the consciousness of created being.

3. *The Demonology of Jesus*

I. Introduction

Biblical scholars have generally neglected the demonology of Jesus, despite the important role it played in his life and thought. According to Mark, Jesus first became famous as an exorciser of demons: "And they were all amazed so that they questioned among themselves, saying 'What is this? A new teaching! With authority he commands even the unclean spirits, and they obey him' " (Mark 1.27). When Luke tells about the return of the seventy disciples, he mentions only one occurrence of their mission, apparently the most remarkable: "The seventy returned with joy, saying, 'Lord, even the demons are subject to us in your name' " (Luke 10.17). Matthew, too, records the amazement of the people when they saw Jesus' power over demons: "And when the demon had been cast out, the dumb man spake; and the crowds marvelled, saying, 'Never was anything like this seen in Israel' " (Matt. 9.33).

In considering the demonology of Jesus, we shall utilize terms from theology and psychoanalysis, but let it be understood from the beginning that we shall not strictly adhere to these disciplines. No self-respecting theologian or psychoanalyst would be satisfied with the methods of this essay. The theologian would argue that we have neglected a spiritual plane of existence which wholly transcends Jesus' apparent human personality. The psycho-analyst would assert that since adequate information about Jesus' psychic condition is wanting, he must forever remain unanalyzed. Since, in the absence of complete data, we indeed cannot psycho-analyze Jesus the man, this investigation will focus upon an analysis of Jesus the image. This image, as represented in the New Testament, has meant so much to religion in the western world, that any insight we might gain might also usefully serve as a commentary on the men who have sought to conform their lives to its form and substance.

II. Sources

In this exploration of the demonology of Jesus, the synoptic gospels will be the principal source. While differing greatly in other respects, their representations of demonology are remarkably similar. There are forty-one references to Satan or evil spirits (or their synonyms) in Matthew, thirty-nine in Mark, and fifty-one in Luke; the differences in quantity are proportionate to the differing length of the gospels themselves. The synoptic gospels seem also to agree in their emphasis upon demon exorcism; there are six such accounts: (1) the first healing, the man in the synagogue with unclean spirit (Mark 1.23-27, Luke 4.33-6); (2) the wild Gadarene whose demon Jesus chases into the swine (Mark 5.1-21, Matt. 8.28-34, Luke 8.26-40); (3) the dumb and possibly blind man who is healed preceding accusations against him by the priests (Matt. 9.32-3, Matt. 12.33, Luke 11.14); (4) the daughter of the Syro-Phoenician woman (Mark 7.25-30, Matt. 15.22-8); (5) the epileptic youth whom the disciples had failed to heal (Mark 9.14-29, Matt. 17.14-21, Luke 9.37-42); and (6) the woman whose back is bent by Satan (Luke 13.11-16). If, as in the usual gospel criticism, one divides the sources into Mark "Q" (that source which Matthew and Luke contain apart from Mark), and "L" (the source used exclusively by Luke), then each source must be given the exclusive rights to at least one story); moreover, one must also acknowledge that each gospel omits something of the others. Thus Matthew omits the first healing in the synagogue while Luke omits the healing of the Syro-Phoenician's daughter. For this reason, we shall not attempt to differentiate strictly between source documents, but shall consider these three gospels as more or less a single source document for the demonology of Jesus.

John gives no clear-cut account of demon exorcism by Jesus, but he does indicate that Jesus was aware of the phenomenon of demoniacal possession: "The Jews answered him, 'Are we not right in saying that you are a Samaritan and have a demon?' Jesus answered, 'I have not a demon, but I honor my Father and you dishonor me' " (John 8.48-9). The author of John, who seems to have been well educated, may have disbelieved in demons and omitted accounts of exorcism for this reason. If, on the other hand, he did believe in demon possession, he still might have deemphasized it in order to counter the elaborate beliefs of the gnostics. Paul had to fight such a battle even though he appears to have believed in demons himself. In writing to the Colossians, Paul warns against over-emphasizing angelology: "Let no man beguile you of your reward in a voluntary humility and worshipping of angels, intruding into those things which he hath not seen, vainly puffed up by his fleshly mind" (Coloss. 2.18).

Whereas John at least mentions the demonology of Jesus in passing, Paul gives it no consideration at all in his epistles. Thus we are left with the synoptic gospels for our major source. One might, however, argue against their "objectivity" by attempting to prove that the gospel writers, who wrote in Greek, had attributed a fundamentally Greek demonology to the Hebrew Jesus without warrant or reason. But this speculation leads nowhere; and, as will be pointed out later, Greek demonology is much less similar to that of Jesus' than is his own Hebraic demonology. In any case, possible Greek influences upon this aspect of Jesus' personality will be discounted.

III. Terminology

The Synoptic gospels contain fifty-three references to *"daimonia."* *Daimonion* was originally the Greek word for god and it occurs five times as such in the *Iliad*. Later on, the word came to be used only for intermediary gods, and by the time of the gospels, its reference had been restricted to evil gods. Thus we may consider it as synonymous with another Greek term which appears twice in Luke, *"pneuma ponera"* or evil spirit. A third term is used synonymously with these in the gosepls: *"pneuma akatharta"* or unclean spirit. Unclean spirit (as a phrase) appears thirteen times in Mark, while Matthew and Luke do not use it as often (twice and six times respectively) and John fails to use it all. Why, one may ask, should a demon be described as unclean? There is little literary precedence for this New Testament term: the Old Testament has only one reference to it in Zechariah 13.2, and Greek literature does not appear to contain it at all.

Satan, the devil, Beelzebul, the prince of demons, the prince of the world, the evil one, the tempter, and the enemy—all these words are used more or less interchangeably to designate the chief demon. *"Satanas"* is not a Greek word as have been the words considered thus far; instead, it is Hebrew. It occurs three times in the Old Testament: first in the temptation of King David to number his armies (I Chron. 21.1), second in the scene before God in Job (Job 1.6), and third in a passage in the book of Zechariah (3.1). Satan was originally a common noun meaning adversary, but during the course of Jewish literature, it became restricted in its meaning to the chief demon exclusively. *"Diabolos,"* based upon the Greek word "to slander" and meaning "the slanderer," is used synonymously with Satan in the gospels. This meaning of the word does not appear anywhere in previous Greek literature. *"Diabolos"* appears six times in Matthew and a like number in Luke, but is absent altogether from Mark, even though Matthew and Luke insert the word into passages paralleling Mark. The King James Version causes some confusion by translating both *"diabolos'* and *"daimonion"* as "demon."

Beelzebul is spelled "beelzeboul', in the original Greek of the New Testament but for some reason was mis-translated by the Latin Vulgate into "Belzebub." The word can be traced back to its Hebrew roots in the words "Ba'al" (lord) plus "zebul" (house, or alternatively, filth). Apparently, at the time of Jesus, the compound word meant lord of filth, since Jesus may be punning its former meaning in Matthew 10.25: "If they have called the master of the house Beelzebul, how much more will they malign those of his household?" A similar word appears once in the Old Testament (II Kings, first chapter) where King Ahaziah is sent to "Baalzebub, the God of Ekron" to see whether he would recover

from a certain disease. Here the King James spelling of the translation is correct and means "lord of the flies." It may be suggested
that this is the probable origin of the Vulgate mis-translation of
Beelzebul.

In the gospel according to John, three references to "the ruler
of this world" (Greek: *archon tou kosmou*) may be found. This
term is not used in the synoptic gospels, but it is quite similar to
"the prince of demons" (*archonti ton daimonion*) which was
quoted above from Mark.

A problem is raised by the two references of Matthew to "the
evil one" as a synonym for Satan. Each occurs in the explanation
of a parable about sowing seed: "the evil one [Greek: *o poneros*]
comes and snatches away what is sown in his heart" (Matt. 13.19);
and somewhat later in Matt. 13.38: "the good seed means the
sons of the evil one, [Greek: *tou ponerou*] and the enemy who
sowed them is the devil." The problem is this: these two
citations refer beyond doubt to a personage who is meant to
correspond to Satan. In fact, the second one includes *"diabolos"*
in the next line, and the first one parallels the words *"diabolos"*
and *"satanas,"* which are used instead in the corresponding
passages from Luke and Mark. But how are we to interpret these
next two passages from Matthew: "Let what you say be simply
'Yes' or 'No'; anything more than this comes from evil [*tou
ponerou*]" (5.37); and "lead us not into temptation, but deliver
us from evil [*tou ponerou*]" (6.13). Is Matthew here speaking
about Satan? Or is he purposely avoiding such a personification
of evil? Since Matthew does consider "the evil one" to be Satan in
previous contexts, we would seem justified in considering it so here.
And even the gospel of John has Jesus speak similar words prior to
Gethsemane: "I do not pray that thou shouldst take them out of
the world, but that thou shouldst keep them from the evil one
[Greek: *tou ponerou*]" (John 17.15).

IV. Old Testament Demonology

It has been pointed out earlier that Satan appears only three
times in the Old Testament, and that unclean spirits appear only
once. It is especially significant that these three appearances of
Satan take place not in hell, but in heaven; the Old Testament

conception of Satan is not that of the ruler of an underworld diametrically opposed to God, but instead of a "fallen angel" who
still appears to be on speaking terms with God: "Now there was a
day when the sons of God came to present themselves before the
Lord, and Satan came also among them" (Job 1.6).

With regard to the image of Satan in the form of a serpent, the
idea of spirits taking on reptilian shapes is not an uncommon one
in primitive demonologies, and Numbers 21.6 seems to show the
traces of ceremonies to ward them off: "And the Lord sent fiery
serpents among the people, and they bit the people; and much people of Israel died . . . and the Lord said unto Moses, Make thee a
fiery serpent, and set it upon a pole; and it shall come to pass, that
everyone that is bitten, when he looketh upon it, shall live." The
serpent of Genesis 2, however, who tempts Eve just as Satan does
Jesus, was not equated with Satan until after the time of Jesus.

In Isaiah, the vengeance of God will turn cities into waste lands
filled with evil spirits. The coming destruction of Babylon is described in 13.21 (KJV) as follows: "But wild beasts of the desert
shall lie there: and their houses shall be full of doleful creatures;
and owls shall dwell there, and satyrs shall dance there. And the
wild beasts of the islands shall cry in their desolate houses, and
dragons in their pleasant palaces."

It must be admitted that the quotations mentioned above
throw little, if any, light on New Testament demonology in view
of the fact that there are no references to evil spirits causing
madness and dumbness, no rites of exorcism, no hell ruled over
by Satan and his angels, no apocalyptic prediction of the overthrow of Satan by the Messiah. There is, however, one reference
to the exorcism of an evil spirit in the Old Testament, but surpris-
ingly enough this evil spirit is sent directly from God. As I Samuel
16.23 records: "And it came to pass, when the evil spirit from God
was upon Saul, that David took an harp, and played with his hand:
so Saul was refreshed and was well, and the evil spirit departed
from him." God speaks with Satan about Job; God sends the evil
spirit to descend upon Saul; God tells Moses how to combat the
fiery serpents; God turns offending cities into the habitations of
evil spirits. This, in short, is a remarkable illustration of how the
Old Testament reconciles an inevitable recurrence of demonology
with the requirements that there be only one God, for if and when

evil spirits do appear in the Israelite world, they must be directly answerable to God.

V. Persian Demonology

The dualism of Zoroastrianism has traditionally been considered the chief influence upon Hebrew demonology at the time of Jesus. One Persian concept, in particular the idea of a kingdom of evil ruled by a chief demon and opposed diametrically to a kingdom of the good is quite similar to the New Testament opposition between God and Satan. But perhaps the most striking similarity between Persian and New Testament ideas is that between the temptations of Zoroaster and Jesus. As Edward Langton has written:

> First it is said Angra Mainyu [the head of the kingdom of evil] sent the demon Buitu to kill Zoroaster. But the prophet chanted aloud the Ahuna-Vairyu formula, and the demon fled back to Angra Mainyu. Then Angra Mainyu himself assailed the prophet. He offered to bestow upon him the sovereignty of the worlds if he would only renounce the good religion of the worshippers of Mazda. But the prophet resisted the temptation and affirmed that neither for body nor life would he do the bidding of Angra Mainyu.[1]

The Persians, like many other cultures including the Babylonians, Arabians, Assyrians, and Egyptians, had elaborate beliefs in various local demons who could inflict disease, suffering, and death upon those who did not take adequate precautions. Thus there were many rites of exorcism and protection from demons in the cultures surrounding Galilee, and it would be difficult, if not impossible, to trace single lines of development from one to another.

VI. Apocalyptic Demonology

Demonology is especially well developed in the apocryphal and apocalyptic writings before and during the time of Jesus. The most extensive and interesting references may be found in the following texts: Tobit (c. 175 B.C.), I Enoch (c. 170-110 B.C.), Jubilees (c. 135-105 B.C.), and I Enoch, chaps. 37-71, 91-104 (c. 95-64 B.C.). Tobit gives an account of an evil spirit named Asmodeus who had slain the first seven husbands of Sarah. The archangel Raphael saves Tobias, her eighth husband, from this fate by exorcising the demon. Raphael's magic powers here are related to his use of the heart and liver of a fish: "Tobias remembered what Raphael had said, and took the ashes of the incense and put the heart and the liver of the fish on them and made a smoke. And when the demon smelled the smoke, he fled to the farthest parts of Upper Egypt, and the angel bound him there."[2]

I Enoch, which often refers to demonology, is made up of many small sections written by different authors at different times; thus many of the stories are at variance with each other. In one of several stories about the origins of evil, Semjaza and Azazel lead a conspiracy of angels who descend to the earth and marry the daughters of men. The offspring of this marriage are giants, whose offspring, in turn, are the evil spirits who are to plague mankind until the final judgment, when they will be destroyed. (It seems plausible that this story is an elaboration upon Genesis 6.2-5, where the "sons of God saw the daughters of men that they were fair; and they took them wives of all.") In the two accounts of the fall of the angels (I Enoch 21,86), the fall is metaphorically described in terms of falling stars. Such an idea may well be represented in the following words of Jesus in Luke 10.18: "And he said unto them, I behold Satan as lightning fall from Heaven."

Although Satan is one of the figures among the fallen angels in the stories of I Enoch, he is far from the dominant one. At various times, one discovers Semjaza, Azazel, and whole classes of Satans as rulers over the forces of evil. The most important contribution of I Enoch to the demonology of Jesus is the prediction of the destruction of Satan's kingdom by the Messiah. Two references may be cited; the first from 54.6, the second from 69.27-8: "And Michael, and Gabriel, and Raphael, and Phanuel shall take hold of them on that great day, and cast them on that day into the burning furnace, that the Lord of Spirits may take vengeance on them for their unrighteousness in becoming subject to Satan and leading astray those who dwell on the earth." "And he sat on the throne of his glory, And the sum of judgment was given unto the

Son of Man. And he caused the sinners to pass away and be destroyed from off the face of the earth, And those who have led the world astray. With chains shall they be bound, And in their assemblage-place of destruction shall they be imprisoned, And all their works vanish from the face of the earth."

Jubilees often echoes the ideas of Enoch, including an account of the fall of the angels and the presence of a tempter who opposes God and is called alternately Mastema and Satan. The most important idea relating to Jesus is the following eschatological prediction: "And all their days they will complete and live in peace and in joy, And there will be no Satan nor any evil destroyer; For all their days will be days of blessing and healing. And at that time the Lord will heal his servants And they will rise up and see great peace, And drive out their adversaries" (Jubilees 23: 29-30). This passage is unique in its prediction not only of the destruction of Satan, but also of the healing of all disease. To be sure, Messianic expectation was current at the time of Jesus, but whether or not it was equated with demons causing disease is much more debatable.

VII. Greek Demonology

The nature and development of Greek demonology is a controversial issue. Selby McCasland, investigating the demon exorcism of Jesus in his book, *By the Finger of God,* declares that he is unable to find significant Greek references in the first century to disease-causing evil spirits: "So far as I have been able to discover, there is not a single authentic Greek or Roman document of the first century, except the New Testament, which shows a case of demon possession and exorcism. Probably the greatest authority on first century Greek religion is Pausanias. He gives an elaborate account of Greek shrines, beliefs, miracle stories, and divine healing of disease, but not a word about demon possession and exorcism. . . ."[3] On the other hand, Edward Langton in his *Essentials of Demonology* finds much to discuss: "Among the Greeks, as elsewhere, a numerous class of demons is composed of departed human spirits which, for various reasons, are thought to have become hostile to the living. By the time of the classical writers some of these spirits seem to have developed into gods of the underworld. . . ."[4] Langton continues:

> The ghosts or spirits called Keres, of which the Greek thus thought to rid themselves, were pictured as tiny winged creatures. Numerous representations of them have been found on the vase paintings of the period. . . . All kinds of physical ills are traceable to the action of Keres, for example blindness and madness. By the Greeks, as by the Babylonians and Assyrians, the sensation of nightmare was attributed to a demon.

This controversy may be important for the students of Greek demonology as such, but for the purposes of biblical criticism it seems immaterial. Matthew, Mark, Luke, and John do not speak of "Keres." The New Testament Satan does not resemble the gods of the Greek underworld nearly as much as do earlier Persian and Jewish apocalyptic demons. Even the words used by the gospel writers are either taken from Hebrew (Satan, Beelzebul, and the special use of "diabolos") or else have the same connotations as Hebrew words (demon, evil and unclean spirits, etc.).

VIII. Demonology Contemporary to Jesus

So far I have considered the effects of Old Testament, Persian, Apocalyptic, and Greek demonologies upon those of the time of Jesus. There appears to have been a continuous conflict of sorts between the attempt to limit the Jewish beliefs to one God and the tendency to absorb various demonological beliefs from neighboring cultures, especially a fundamental good-evil dualism from Persia. In addition, there appears to have been a tendency strictly within educated Jewish circles to return to and rewrite pre-Mosaic traditions of demonological monsters and fallen angels, etc., and thereby illuminate and ascertain the origins of the kingdom of evil which the coming Messiah would destroy. Among the less educated classes, there was probably a tendency to practice magical rites, such as demon exorcism, which were common in neighboring countries.

We can learn a great deal about first-century Jewish beliefs from the New Testament itself. It cannot be over-emphasized that despite great efforts made by the chief priests to find charges to bring against Jesus, it is not once stated that Jesus commits heresy by acknowledging Satan and demon possession. There is, however, one hint of such talk in the passage from Mark 3:22: "And the scribes who came down from Jerusalem said, 'He is possessed by Beelzebul, and by the prince of demons he casts out the demons.' " Even if the two statements are meant to be casually connected, the simple implication is that Jesus must be mad in order to *cast out* demons. The notion that Jesus must be mad for he recognizes demons is not implied at all. Jesus counters this charge in the corresponding passage from Mark 1:27: "And if I cast out demons by Beelzebul, by whom do your sons cast them out?" It appears from this, that the exorcism of demons was not an uncommon practice in Israel. It was apparently not forbidden by the priests; for if the priests themselves practiced exorcism as Jesus charges, and yet forbade its practice by others, why does Jesus fail to mention this in his many charges of hypocrisy?

Mention is made of other Jewish exorcists in Mark 9:38, Luke 9:49, and Acts 19:13. In each of these cases, the exorcist uses the name of Jesus. Does this mean that such exorcism sprang up in the wake of the success of Jesus? Or had it existed all along? The charge by Jesus that the sons of the Pharisees cast out demons seems to indicate that it existed all along. Yet Jesus seems to be unique among Jewish exorcists: "And when the demon had been cast out, the dumb man spoke; and the crowds marvelled, saying, Never was anything like this seen in Israel" (Matthew 9:33).

Since Jesus was not the only exorcist the people had seen, his uniqueness must lie in other sources. For one thing, many exorcists might well have been operating in his neighborhood, but they were probably much less successful than he. The very success of Jesus was unique. For another thing, primitive methods of demon exorcism rely upon elaborate rites consisting of magic words, magic gestures, and special instruments, and Jesus was probably unique in his independence from these means. Josephus, the Jewish historian who died in 95 A.D., gives the following account of an exorcism performed by a Jew named Eleazor before the emperor Vespasian:

> The manner of the cure was this: He put a ring that has a root of one of those sorts mentioned by Solomon to the nostrils of the demoniac, after which he drew out the demon through his nostrils; and when the man fell down immediately, he adjured him to return unto him no more, making still mention of Solomon, and reciting the incantations which he composed. And when Eleazor would persuade and demonstrate to the spectators that he had such power, he set a little way off a cup or basin full of water, and commanded the demon, as he went out of the man, to overturn it, and thereby to let the spectators know that he had left the man (*Antiquities,* VIII, ii, 5).

Unlike Eleazor, Jesus need only say "Hold thy peace, and come out of him," and the demon departs. To be sure, we are still dealing with a magic phrase, but it is so unpretentious that the "authority" of Jesus must be of a new and remarkable kind.

There are vestiges of magical practice in the healing of the Gadarene. In this case, Jesus asks the demon for his name and receives the answer "My name is Legion." Anyone familiar with accounts of primitive magic will recognize the high magical value attached to possessing the name of a demon. After being cast out, the demons flee from the Gadarene into the herd of swine. Here again we find a typical primitive belief in the transference of qualities from one object to another. Each of these two magical devices is also used in the ritual of Eleazor mentioned above. In general, however, Jesus works without any emphasis upon ritual. The account of the healing of the Gadarene, which constitutes the one exception, seems so scientifically unlikely that we have some justification for attributing it to a folk tale which crept into the "memories" of Jesus. The conditions which Jesus imposes upon the father of the epileptic boy whom he heals are more in character: "If thou canst believe, all things are possible." And what kind of ritual could have been performed upon the daughter of the Syro-Phoenician woman whom Christ healed without even seeing?

NEW TESTAMENT DEMONOLOGY IN GENERAL

I. Importance for Jesus

References to evil spirits and to Satan creep and intrude into every aspect of the speech and activities of Jesus. Out of the twenty or so healings affected by him in the synoptic gospels, six of these are by the exorcism of demons. There are references to Jesus performing many exorcisms of demons in the crowds of people that followed him (Mark 1:34, 39; 3:12; 16:9; Matt. 4:24; 8:16; Luke 4:41; 6:18; 7:21; 8:2; 13:31). Among the parables spoken by Jesus, three have direct reference to Satan or to unclean spirits (Mark 4:14; Matt. 12:43; 13:19,38; Luke 8:12; 11:24). Jesus begins his ministry after temptations by Satan (Mark 1:13; Matt. 4:1; Luke 4:1), and during the course of the gospels, Judas (Luke 22:3; John 6:70; 13:27), Peter (Mark 8:33; Matt. 16:23; Luke 22:31), and John the Baptist (Matt. 11:18; Luke 7:33) are all mentioned in conjunction with evil spirits or Satan. The original version of the Lord's Prayer concluded with the words "deliver us from evil" (Matt. 6:13; Luke 11:4). The Last Supper with the disciples includes a prayer to "keep them from the evil one" (John 17:15). And, perhaps most important of all, the greatest power Jesus gives to his disciples is the ability to cast out demons (Mark 3:15; 6:7,13; 16:17; Matt. 10:1,8; Luke 9:1; 10:17).

Before the role of demonology in the life of Jesus is considered, some time will be given to the characteristics of evil spirits and Satan in general. It will be the attempt of the succeeding pages to provide answers for the following questions:

(1) Why are evil spirits called unclean? The term "unclean spirit" appears eighteen times in the gospels.

(2) Why do demons scream and have to be silenced? "Jesus rebuked him, saying, 'Be silent, and come out of him!' And the unclean spirit, convulsing him and crying with a loud voice, came out of him" (Mark 1:26). "And demons also came out of many, crying, 'You are the Son of God!' But he rebuked them, and would not allow them to speak. . . ." (Luke 4:41).

(3) Why does demon possession cause dumbness and blindness?

"Then a blind and dumb demoniac was brought to him, and he healed him, so that the dumb man spoke and saw" (Matt. 12:22).

(4) Why do demons thrash about or fall down and have to be bound with chains? "And when the spirit saw him, immediately it convulsed the boy, and he fell on the ground and rolled about, foaming at the mouth" (Mark 9:20). "And unclean spirits, when they saw him, fell down before him, and cried. . . ." (Mark 3:10-1). "The chains he wrenched apart, and the fetters he broke in pieces" (Mark 5:4).

(5) Why do evil spirits wear no clothes and live in tombs, swine, and deserts? "There met him a man from the city who had demons; for a long time he had worn no clothes, and he lived not in a house but among the tombs" (Luke 8:27). "And the unclean spirits came out, and entered the swine" (Mark 5:13). "When the unclean spirit has gone out of a man he passes through waterless places. . . ." (Matt. 12:43).

(6) Why do many devils replace the one in a parable? "Then he goes and brings seven other spirits more evil than himself, and they enter and dwell there; and the last state of that man becomes worse than the first" (Luke 11:26).

(7) What is the power behind the words with which Jesus rids himself of Satan's temptation?: "He turned and said to Peter, 'Get thee behind me, Satan!' " (Matt. 16:23).

(8) Why is Satan associated with a fiery hell? "Depart from me, you cursed, into the eternal fire prepared for the devil and his angels" (Matt. 25:41).

II. A Theoretical Statement

What is the origin of demons? Freud tackles this problem in *Totem and Taboo*, considering only those demons derived from the spirits of the departed:

> We now know how to explain the supposed demonism of recently departed souls and the necessity of being protected against their hostility through taboo rules . . . hostility, which is painfully felt in the unconscious in the form of satisfaction with the demise, experiences a different fate in the case of primitive man: the defense against it is

accomplished by displacement upon the object of the
hostility, namely the dead. We call this defense process,
frequent both in normal and diseased life, a projection.
The survivors will deny that they have ever entertained
hostile impulses toward the beloved dead; but now the soul
of the deceased entertains them and will try to give vent to
them. . . .[5]

Freud's remarks here are so pertinent to our topic that we will
let him repeat himself in different words:

This unknown hostility, of which we are ignorant and of
which we do not wish to know, is projected from our inner
perception into the outer world and is thereby detached
from our own person and attributed to the other. Not we,
the survivors, rejoice because we are rid of the deceased,
on the contrary, we mourn for him; but now curiously
enough, he has become an evil demon who would rejoice
in our misfortune and who seeks our death. The survivors
must now defend themselves against this evil enemy; they
are freed from inner oppression, but they have only succeeded in exchanging it for an affliction from without.[6]

Thus far, Freud has considered only those demons derived from
deceased men, a subject which he worked with at some length in
Totem and Taboo. But in another paper much closer to our
subject matter, he speaks of demoniacal possession in general:

Cases of demoniacal possession correspond to the neuroses
of the present day; in order to understand these latter we
have once more had recourse to the conception of psychic
forces. What in those days were thought to be evil spirits to
us are base and evil wishes, the derivatives of impulses
which have been rejected and repressed. In one respect only
do we not subscribe to the explanation of these phenomena
current in mediaeval times; we have abandoned the
projection of them into the outer world, attributing their
origin instead to the inner life of the patient in whom
they manifest themselves.[7]

Let us conclude our theoretical statements with remarks by two of the leading psychoanalysts since Freud. Unlike Freud, they are child analysts, and through daily therapeutic contact with children, they are more familiar than most with the human origins of evil and the means of coping with it. For Erik Erikson, "the mechanisms of projection and introjection . . . remain some of our deepest and most dangerous defense mechanisms. In introjection, we feel and act as if an outer goodness had become an inner certainty. In projection, we experience an inner harm as an outer one: we endow significant people with the evil which actually is in us."[8] And Anna Freud: "the use of the mechanism of projection is quite natural to the ego of little children throughout the earliest period of infancy. They employ it as a means of repudiating their own activities and wishes when these become dangerous and of laying the responsibility for them at the door of some external agent."[9]

Before continuing the textual criticism, let us ask what impulses might be so evil that one would wish to deny them by projecting them onto evil spirits. Hostility, murder, slander? These are obvious, and Satan is obviously the embodiment of them. But what can one say of those forms of evil which are exhibited by children and, despite their having been repressed, remain in the adult's unconscious mind? What if an infant wishes to put his hand into the attractive flames of the stove? What if an infant screams too loud and long? But why be so selective? Why not choose a dozen other types of badness which would have much less to do with the biblical evil spirits? This important question will be reconsidered after the subject of demonology in Scripture has been approached from several more angles.

The reader is aware that human behavior is being greatly simplified in these considerations of the projection of evil. People do not spend all of their time projecting evil in the same way that they eat food regularly. But such constant preoccupation with evil is not at all necessary to our thesis. If everyone, *at one time or another*, projects such impulses as we are considering here, then this is sufficient cause not only to give evil spirits the traits which they possess, but also to insure our unconscious recognition of their significance. Such projection as we are considering takes place mostly in childhood and in extremely unstable adult mental

conditions. The former insures that all of us will recognize an
evil spirit when we see one; the latter we may wish to apply to the
case of Jesus.

III. The Nature of Evil Spirits

We have already begun to answer questions (1), (2), (4),
and (8). If demons represent, as we have said, the denial of evil
impulses by projection, then it follows that among their characteristics should be uncleanliness, offensive screaming, thrashing
about, and fascination with fire. We can also include in this
category the nakedness of the Gadarene (5). He should, of
course, be clothed. But let us consider uncleanliness on a more
general level. "Unclean and evil" has often been contrasted with
"clean and good." The ancient Hebrews couched their dietary
restrictions in terms of clean and unclean foods. Freudian analysis
is especially interested in the conjunction of dirt and feces on the
one hand, versus cleanliness and bowel control, on the other
(compare "Beelzebul" which means "Lord of filth" in the sense
of excrement). At a later stage, there is a contrast between dirt
and sex and cleanliness and sublimation of sex (for example in
the idiomatic "dirty stories"). If anything, we are burdened with
a surplus of explanations for "unclean spirits." But the gospel
writers may have had all these things in mind.

Dream analysis has shown how one often condenses a whole
series of meaning into a single symbol. This would also help to
answer the question raised above as to why Jesus chose only a few
selected impulses to project onto demons. "Unclean" thus, stands
not only for itself, but also for the evils of eating improper things,
failing to control the bowels, manifesting sexual excitement
at improper times, etc.

Questions (2) and (3) on our list are exact opposites. Why
are evil spirits so often described as screaming offensively and
also as remaining absolutely dumb? One can offer a common
sense explanation: Demon possesson implies loss of control over
one's self; therefore, one loses the ability to control his speech
and either screams or remains dumb. But let us see if there is not
a better explanation.

First, consider the list of demons in the verse Isaiah 13:21

quoted earlier. The KJV has rather badly misquoted the Hebrew in this case. The Hebrew word translated as satyrs is "Seirim" which in various Old Testament references appears to be either a goat or a calf. The word's etymology implies simply "hairy." The Hebrew word "Ziyyim"—which is translated as "wild beasts"— does not denote any particular animal but may be translated as either "desert-dweller" or "crier." Both meanings compare especially well with characteristics of demons in the New Testament. The Hebrew word "Ochim," which is translated as "doleful creatures" comes from a root meaning "to cry" or "to howl" and does not name any particular animal. The Hebrew word "Iyyim," which is mistranslated as "wild beasts of the islands" again comes from the root of "to howl" or "to screech." And the last word, "Tannin" in Hebrew, which is mistranslated as "dragons," again comes from a root meaning "to howl." The one word that we have not mentioned, "owls," which seems to fit nicely into the above pattern, is also a mistranslation. The Hebrew "Benoth ya' anah" does not mean "screaming," but it carries a connotation of evil nonetheless; it means "daughters of greed." The idea of demons as screaming creatures is thus an old one and is not confined to the New Testament.

Sometimes, dumbness and blindness are caused by evil spirits; at other times, by the spirit of the Lord. For example, notice that Simeon is struck dumb by the angel Gabriel and that Paul is struck blind by the vision of Jesus. Uncontrolled speaking and screaming are attributed to those possessed by the spirit of God as well as by demons (divinations, tongues, etc.). Thus we find a fundamental ambivalence, not only between screaming and dumbness as two opposite effects of the same causative agent, the evil spirit, but also between two opposite agents, spirits of good and spirits of evil. To avoid this complexity, one could try to set the problem. Demons scream, we noted earlier, because human beings are equal in the unconscious. But let us not be so quick to drop the problem. Demons scream, we noted earlier, because human beings defend themselves against the desire to scream by projecting such an impulse onto them. But projection is not the only defence mechanism. Negation or denial is another. If screaming is a projection of an evil impulse, then dumbness is the projection of the denial of this impulse. Until the nature of a "defence mechanism" is considered, this answer sounds, and is, ridiculous; this much may be said: the farther we remove an impulse from being recogniz- able, the better is the defence. Thus, the projection of a denial is an excellent defence. The question, "Why do both good and evil spirits cause the same effects?" cannot be thoroughly explored, for to attempt to answer this question would lead us too far afield from the problem of evil spirits and involve us in an investigation of the functions of good spirits. It must be left as the starting point for a further study.

Question (4) refers to the frequency of demons falling down, on the one hand, and being bound, on the other. Here again is a pair of apparently opposite effects stemming from the same source. Mark 3:10-1 has caused no little perturbation among Biblical scholars. *The Interpreter's Bible*, for example, comments: "It has been proposed to place a period after 'touch him' in vs. 10 and to read the rest of the verse with what follows: 'As many as had plagues and unclean spirits.' This would somehow relieve the strain upon the modern reader, who finds it impossible really to conceive of unclean spirits as beholding, falling down, etc.; but the suggested punctuation destroys the distinction that Mark made between the sick persons in vs. 10 and the demons in vs. 11."

Other verses in the gospels refer to the convulsing effect of demons (Mark 1:26 and Luke 4:35). One should note that the woman with the bent back has been "bound" by Satan. Is it co- incidental that Satan requires Jesus to "fall down and worship me"? We have read in apocalyptic literature how the powers of evil "fell" from heaven. When the demon who had afflicted Sarah fled to Egypt, "the angel bound him there." Enoch promises that "those who have led the world astray. With chains shall they be bound." The man whom Eleazor healed of a demon "fell down immediately." One is reminded here of the common custom of swaddling infants to keep them from injuring themselves with their uncontrolled movements. Thrashing about or convulsive behavior would be more or less "bad" behavior at this stage and a child would be bound to keep him from it. In this context, the binding of evil spirits may be considered as the projection of the denial of an impulse.

We have referred to falling down as the opposite of being bound, but is this true? In order to fall down, one must be able to walk or at least to stand up. When the infant fears punishment, he will deny his evil by falling down, regressing to the stage when he could not walk. It seems most likely, then, that falling down, like being bound, is the denial of evil impulses; and coordinately, that demons who fall down have regressed to a stage where they are harmless. But let us digress briefly, and turn the table on psychoanalysis by inspecting its own terminology. Freud and his followers speak of the necessity of delaying responses to stimuli before the infant can gain muscular control. The terminology is to "bind a cathexis"—cathexis meaning roughly "mental energy." According to Otto Fenichel, "The mastery of the motor apparatus, too, is a task that the human infant only gradually learns . . . through the interposing of a time period between stimulus and reaction, by the acquisition of a certain tension tolerance, that is, of an ability to bind primitive reaction impulses by countercathexes."[10] Like primitive thought which considers the soul as a "little man" inside the big man, psychoanalysis seems to envisage cathexis as "little babies inside the big baby" which must be bound just as the infant himself is bound.

Question (5) considers the dwelling places of demons. Tombs are to be expected. As Freud notes in *Totem and Taboo*, the first evil spirits were probably the spirits of the departed, and one would especially be reminded of them around the tombs. Such a belief is not at all limited to the primitive mind; many of our modern mystery and horror stories take place in graveyards. Swine, too, are an especially appropriate dwelling place for the demons of the Gadarene. Not only are these animals universally considered greedy and filthy, but for the Jews they were restricted from the diet as well and called "unclean." But what about "waterless places"? The belief that demons haunt deserts as well as other out of the way places such as wells, tombs, deep woods, and caves is an old one in primitive demonologies, and many vestiges remain in modern thought. Primitive peoples, children, and sometimes even you and I are afraid of dark corners, the woods at night, etc. Who is there? The creatures of nightmare? The places where no man dwells are where the demons dwell. Then, too, deserts are places where one is thirsty. . . .

Why do many spirits replace one in the parable by Jesus? He seems to imply that "nature abhors a vacuum." If one does not fill

himself with the Holy Spirit, he will find himself filled instead
with evil spirits. It is difficult to resist recalling Cassius' "lean and
hungry look" at this point. The hungry man is the dangerous man.
This is paralleled by the activity of children who will scream,
kick or exhibit some other aggressive behavior when they are
hungry. We have already discussed two other stories which can be
partly elucidated by the relationship between hunger and aggres-
sion. Satan's first temptation is made after Jesus has fasted for
forty days. And demons are especially to be encountered in
waterless places, where one is thirsty.

IV. The Nature of Satan

Only some manuscripts of Luke quote Jesus as telling the
tempting Satan to "Get thee behind me" and Matthew says only
"Get thee hence." On the other hand, both Matthew and Mark
agree as to the wording of Jesus' warning to Peter: "Get thee
behind me, Satan." This can be understood "in view" of the fact
that when someone is standing before you, he is much more
imposing than if he is behind you. Jesus is face to face with Satan,
while God is somewhere in the far distance. Who then is more
real for Jesus, God or Satan? With Satan standing right in front
of Jesus, he tends to seem more real than God. Are then his gifts
and promises more real than those of God? Jesus' doubt in God
must be countered with a remark like "Get thee behind me." At
this point, another passage from Erik Erikson may be usefully
reproduced. For Erickson, "Doubt is the brother of shame.
Where shame is dependent on the consciousness of being upright
and exposed, doubt . . . has much to do with a consciousness of
having a front and a back. . . . For this reverse area of the body . . .
can be dominated by the will of others. The 'Behind' is thus the
individual's dark continent, an area of the body which can be
magically dominated and effectively invaded by those who would
attack one's powers of autonomy. . . ." [11] Children are thus made
to learn that the part of the body which they cannot see is "evil."
In this context, the "behind" is where Satan actually belongs.
Were he to come around and face us, then our entire body, not
just our "behind," would be in danger of becoming evil. Was Jesus

ever in danger, it must be asked, of being wholly overcome by his own evil impulses?

One question remains. Why is Satan associated with a fiery hell? It has already been suggested that Satan embodies, among other forbidden impulses, the desire to play with fire. Apocalyptic literature (cf. Enoch 54:6) makes many references to a fiery hell where evil spirits will eventually be destroyed. Satan and his angels are to be bound and cast into a fiery furnace. In the book of Daniel, Shadrach, Meshach, and Abednego are bound and cast into a fiery furnace for refusing to worship the king's idols. In this story, despite the death of those who threw them into the fire, the victims remain magically unscorched. This is a more straightforward projection of the desire to play with fire. And perhaps the scriptural hell is related in some way to the projection of such a forbidden impulse onto evil spirits who will be punished there.

Instead of such a general approach, one can take an historical one by considering the origins of the Hebrew word "Gehenna," which we know by translation as "hell." Derived from the "ge Hinnom" of Joshua 15:8, the name identifies the valley of Hinnom near Jerusalem where human sacrifices had once been offered. Such a valley answers well to requirements for the habitation of demons. It is unclean and uninhabitable. In this sense, the word for hell derives strictly from the local experience of the Israelites, and does not assist the student of comparative primitive beliefs.

A THEORY OF THE PERSONALITY OF JESUS

I. Preliminary Remarks

Before the personality of Jesus is considered, it may be beneficial to review some objections raised as to the methodology of our investigation. Can we consider Jesus as an historical figure and the gospels as an accurate account of his life and saying? Would it not be better to consider only a "core of truth" in the gospels and reject the rest as a posteriori speculation? We have already remarked that this essay can only speculate about Jesus and that the only material which it can use is the gospel accounts. As for the second question, who is to decide what part of the gospels is a "core of truth"? Such decisions are necessarily biased. For example, most religious commentators would not hesitate to consider the words "Get thee behind me, Satan," as more likely the words of the gospel writers than those of Jesus. To such commentators, the words would not seem significant enough to warrant an exact quotation by the gospel writers. On the other hand, in our investigation, we have considered these words as highly significant, in which case they might well have been quoted accurately. The same reasoning will apply to the words "for a season" in Luke 4:13.

The question was raised earlier as to why evil spirits embody such a wide and seemingly arbitrary range of evil impulses. One could also ask why people must project these forms of badness in the first place? The following pages will attempt to point out the close interdependence of these two questions and their significance for the life of Jesus:

(1) Why does Luke consider the temptation only temporarily concluded? "And when the devil had ended all the temptation, he departed from him for a season" (Luke 4:13).

(2) Why is Jesus accused of having a demon? "And when his friends heard it, they went out to seize him, for they said, 'He is beside himself.' And the scribes who came down from Jerusalem said, 'He is possessed by Beelzebul. . . .' " (Mark 3:21-2). "Many of them said, 'He has a demon, and he is mad; why listen to him?' " (John 10:20).

(3) Why does Jesus once lose his temper? "Whosoever blasphemes against the Holy Spirit never has forgiveness, but is guilty of an eternal sin"—for they said, "He has an unclean spirit" (Mark 3:29-30).

(4) Why does Jesus warn Peter and the disciples against temptation during the Last Supper and Gethsemane? "Watch and pray that you may not enter into temptation; the spirit indeed is willing, but the flesh is weak" (Mark 14:38). "Simon, Simon, behold, Satan demanded to have you, that he might sift you like wheat, but I have prayed for you that your faith may not fail" (Luke 22:31). "I do not pray that thou shouldst take them out of the world, but that thou shouldst keep them from the evil one" (John 17:15).

(5) Why do the demons recognize Jesus as the Son of God? "And demons also came out of many, crying, 'You are the Son of God!' But he rebuked them, and would not allow them to speak, because they knew that he was the Christ" (Luke 4:41).

(6) What made Jesus think that he was the Messiah? "But if it is by the finger of God that I cast out demons, then the kingdom of God has come upon you" (Luke 11:20).

(7) How could Jesus be so good-natured? "But I say to you, Do not resist one who is evil. But if any one strikes you on the right cheek, turn to him the other also" (Matt. 5:39).

(8) What was the relationship between Jesus the Son and God the Father? "And a voice came from heaven, 'Thou are my beloved Son; with thee I am well pleased' " (Mark 1:11). " 'Father, if thou art willing, remove this cup from me; nevertheless not my will, but thine, be done.' And there appeared to him an angel from heaven, strengthening him. And being in agony he prayed more earnestly; and his sweat became like great drops of blood falling down upon the ground" (Luke 22:42-4).

(9) Why did Jesus apparently get himself crucified? " 'Why do you seek to kill me?' The people answered, 'You have a demon! Who is seeking to kill you?' " (John 7:19).

II. Jesus Struggles with Evil

There are probably a great number of theological rationalizations for the lines in Luke which state that Satan departed from Jesus "for a season." (RSV: "until an opportune time.") It is to be noted that Matthew's parallel account contains no such phrase. This is a curious inconsistency. On the one hand, we are presented with what is apparently an allegory to illustrate Jesus conquering Satan; on the other, we are told that the victory was incomplete. If one is going to make use of such allegory, why not make a definitive statement, instead of leaving the most important question unanswered as does Luke? Matthew, of course, has no such trouble; Satan appears to be irrevocably vanquished. There is no manuscript disagreement on either passage. All the manuscripts of Luke contain "for a season," and all the manuscripts of Matthew omit this. This difference is a good starting point for a speculation that Jesus was perpetually haunted by Satan.

Jesus is often accused by his enemies (and even by "his friends" in Mark 3:21) of being possessed by a demon. We have quoted two such references under the question (2) and can point to such passages as John 8:48 and Matt. 10:25. Jesus' apparent possession by demons and his continual struggle with Satan seem to be related. But are they? Demons and Satan cannot be used synonymously. At times, the Jews related the two by considering Satan as the ruler over the kingdom of the demons, and at times it even appears that one can be possessed by Satan himself (for example, Judas). But are the two types of possession identical? Possession by demons produces an illness or madness as such, whereas possession by Satan produces a calculatingly malicious action. The two are related by the idea that the physical and mental illness caused by demon possession are the punishment for the evil committed under the influence of Satan. The terrible and unnatural death of Judas, for example, appears to follow from his betrayal of Jesus at the behest of Satan (Luke 22:3).

At this point, let us digress once more and consider "madness" in general, one form of which is today called psychoneurosis. One of the major authorities on the psychoanalytic theory of neurosis, Otto Fenichel, makes the following statement in his "Initial Essay at a Definition of Neurosis": "Thus we have in psychoneuroses, first a defence of the ego against an instinct, then a conflict between the instinct striving for discharge and the defensive forces of the ego, then a state of damming up, and finally the neurotic symptoms which are distorted discharges as a consequence of the state of damming up—a compromise between the opposing forces."[12] Let us focus special attention on the use of the word "defence" in this quotation. There is nothing pathological about defence as such; in fact, psychoanalytic theory tends to attribute most of what we call valuable character traits to the action of defence mechanism such as repression, sublimation, identification, etc. But what happens if an *inappropriate* defence is used against a seemingly dangerous impulse? And what happens if such a defence mechanism fails at a critical time? These last two questions are essential to the thesis of this essay. So far we have been considering evil spirits as the projection of evil impulses; and there is no reason to consider such projections as pathological. Where, then, is the conflict of which Fenichel speaks? There is no conflict if a defence is successful. It is only when such a defence mechanism as projection or repression *fails* and the original impulse threatens to break through, that the pathological symptom of psychoneurosis results.

Perhaps Jesus repressed as a child a basic and extremely dangerous evil impulse. This is not to say a thought in the instantaneous sense, but rather a thought which would have recurred many times in a certain context of life were it not repressed. And that for some unknown reason, at the age of thirty, this repression weakened; the defence mechanism failed. In order to protect against the impulse, his mind would have resorted to a second line of defence as it were: in this case, projection. Thus Jesus' evil may have been projected onto an external world of demons. But instead of projecting the exact, appropriate evil impulse onto the outer world, which would have rendered it so obvious that the evil would have had to become consciously apparent, he may have projected various other forms of evil in place of it, or as distorted images of it, one might say. This is the proposed answer which we promised to provide for the question about the apparent arbitrariness and lack of motivation for the forms of badness projected onto evil spirits.

The ideas of Jesus about the nature of demons fit in well with those of his contemporaries. Jesus found in the demonology of his time an appropriate outlet for his evil impulses; this was probably why he chose the defence mechanism which he did. The chief difference between the demonology of Jesus and that of his contemporaries lay not in the nature of demon characteristics, but in the extraordinary emotional intensity with which Jesus considered and acted upon these beliefs—just as if they were playing a part in a much more fundamental and personal conflict. We have given unorthodox answers to the first two questions. Instead of discounting the statements of Luke and of the "friends" and enemies of Jesus, that he was often tempted by Satan or that he was possessed by demons, we have tended to agree with them. Our views will be justified if they can elucidate some old problems in a new way.

Question (3) concerns one of the most controversial of all biblical verses. *The Interpreter's Bible* notes that it "has given rise to endless speculation regarding 'the unforgivable sin'." The statement is so unlike the ordinary forgiving attitude of Jesus that the King James translators took it upon themselves to modify the words "guilty of eternal sin" (RSV) into "in danger of eternal damnation." Why should Jesus react in a manner so unlike himself, as he had lost his temper? He seems to have been thrown off balance by the words preceding his curse, the accusation that he was actually possessed by "an unclean spirit." Actually, Jesus was not at all what one could call an "evil" man. On the contrary, he led a most righteous life. But it seems that, at least unconsciously, he thought himself quite evil.

Jesus is so disturbed during the Last Supper and at Gethsemane afterwards that he resembles a neurotic under extreme anxiety. All four accounts of this event indicate that he was struggling with evil. In Mark, the original gospel, Jesus says "My soul is exceeding sorrowful unto death." And he warns Peter to "Watch ye and pray, lest ye enter into temptation." Matthew echoes both these verses; but Luke not only has Jesus warn the disciples of temptation twice instead of once, but also elaborates Jesus' agony with the description of his sweating blood. Luke also adds the words warning Peter that Satan desires him, and indicates that Jesus, as well as Peter, has been wrestling with Satan: "When I was with you day after day in the temple, you did not lay hands on me. But this is your hour, and the power of darkness" (Luke 22:53). And the gospel of John contains a long section in which Jesus prays that the disciples should be delivered from temptation.

Why was Jesus so anxious? We are not yet in a position to answer fully this question. Why do the authors of all four gospels (an usually complete agreement) cite Jesus as warning the disciples to beware of temptation? This question we can answer. One need not read Freud to understand that Jesus was projecting his own internal conflict onto his disciples.

III. The Origin of Jesus' Messianic Self-Awareness

In the section on apocalyptic demonology above, we noted a reference in Jubilees which predicts that there will come a time when Satan will no longer exist and when all of God's servants will be healed in the Messianic kingdom. It is not difficult to imagine that once Jesus had performed some "miraculous" healings, others began to think of him as a Messianic candidate and came to him requesting to be healed. And, of course, if they were indeed healed, they would have been most likely to apotheosize Jesus as the true Messiah. That those who were "possessed by demons" should have uttered such remarks, the gospel writers regarded as proof that supernatural powers regarded Jesus as the Messiah. This aspect of demonology is especially emphasized in the gospel of Mark. But it is suggested that the origin of these stories probably lies in the very real and understandable attitude of those who were healed who, in their anticipation of healing, convinced themselves (and the disciples) that Jesus was the promised Messiah.

All four gospels record that when Jesus was baptized by John the Baptist, the spirit of the Lord descended upon him like a dove and a voice said "This is my beloved son." This is generally accepted as the first realization by Jesus of his Messiahship. We have no reason to doubt that some such remarkable experience occurred before his ministry and set it off. But was one such occurrence enough to give Jesus confidence in himself as a Messiah? When did Jesus become famous?

Mark and Luke (Matthew can be demonstrated to have rearranged their material to fit a literary pattern paralleling the history of Israel) placed the first event of the ministry in the following order: Mark—baptism by John, temptation in the wilderness, teaching in Galilee, calling of four disciples, and the healing of the man with unclean spirit; Luke—baptism of Jesus by John the Baptist, but he is never much concerned with the activities of Satan or with evil spirits, so he does not include these events. Not until after the fifth event in Mark does the fame of Jesus "spread abroad throughout all the region." Luke disagrees and reports such fame after only the second event. For Mark, the determining factor is the successful exorcism of a demon, whereas for Luke it is the teaching of Jesus. We may be justified in throwing the emphasis upon the earlier account of Mark which indicates that demon exorcism made Jesus famous for the first time.

Let us try to reconstruct the story. Jesus, previously unsuspecting his Messiahship, had a strange and moving experience when he was baptized by John the Baptist and at this point was first informed that he was the "Son of God." This announcement

had a profound effect upon him, for "immediately," he went into
the wilderness to wrestle with his problems. Upon returning home,
he discovered that he had acquired strange powers of healing,
especially of exorcising demons. This last occurrence, more than
any other, gave him the confidence to believe he was the Messiah.
The passage from Luke quoted with question (6) indicates that
Jesus was aware of the prevailing attitude that associated Messianic
power with the ability to exorcise demons. Once fame of his healing
abilities had spread, all of the sick people in the surrounding
countryside flocked to him to be healed, calling him the Messiah.
What could be more bolstering to his Messianic self-awareness?

IV. The "Goodness" of Jesus and the Father-Son Relationship

Why should Jesus be so "good"? This question should have
the very highest priority for those who call themselves Christians,
and wish to be like him. And yet, the question is almost never
asked. It always seems to be taken for granted that Jesus was good
"because he was good." Let us attempt to give a more direct
and perhaps more significant answer by employing the psychoanalytic theory of personality. How does one rid himself of evil
impulses? One method is projection. We have seen that Jesus
continually uses this mechanism. First he projected his evil onto
Satan during an experience in the wilderness; then he projected his
evil onto the demons which were possessing the sick who came to
see him. But this was not enough. Not only did he rid himself of
evil in this way, but in his identification with the people who came
to be healed, in his "compassion" upon them, it became imperative
that he rid *them* of evil spirits also. This is a mutually reinforcing
pattern: Jesus healed demoniacs because of his personal
conflict and the demoniacs encouraged him to do so because of
their own hopes. Jesus was the supremely good man, because he
was a supreme master of projection. When someone smites you on
one cheek, project your hostility onto him and let him do it
again! But why was Jesus the supreme master of projection? Why,
more than any other man, did he have to project all his evil onto
demons? The answer to this question lies in the nature of his
relationship to God, the father-son relationship.

The time has come to gather together the loose ends of our

essay. What purpose is served by the temptation of Jesus by Satan? Jesus to be sure had little of material value to gain from a pact with the devil. Earlier, we left the following unanswered: "Was Jesus ever in danger of being wholly overcome by his own evil impulses?" Somewhat later, we referred to "a basic and extremely dangerous evil impulse" which all the other evil impulses projected onto Satan and other demons could have symbolized. We also spoke of "a much more fundamental and personal conflict," which we were not yet ready to investigate. Shortly after, we asked "Why was Jesus so anxious?" We noted that Jesus was profoundly affected by being told that he was the "Son of God." And then we left the question: "Why, more than any other man, did he have to project all his evil onto demons?"

All of these questions fall into place when placed into the context of Jesus' relation with his father. We do not know when the father of Jesus died. We do know this, however: that all four gospels agree upon the first important event in his ministry: "and a voice came from heaven, 'Thou art my beloved Son; with thee I am well pleased" (Mark 1:11). And "immediately" Jesus went into the wilderness and was tempted by Satan. Like all men, Jesus had repressed as a child fantasies of murder toward his father. Around thirty years of age, his repression failed and to cope with the conflict he projected it. Whereas many of us conjure up only one father figure and imbue him with evil, Jesus conjured up two: God and Satan. Jesus was thus able to deny that he had killed his father in two ways: his father was still alive (God) and he had never wanted to kill him anyway (only Satan could be so evil). For the rest of his ministry, this "evil impulse," this "personal conflict," this source of acute anxiety, was projected by Jesus into a war between Satan and God for control of mankind. And Jesus was a son in whom God, the Father, could indeed be "well pleased" since he had fought so well against Satan.

Why did Jesus get himself killed? Did he commit suicide? At any rate, he did not attempt to avoid death. Earlier, it was asked what would happen if the defence that one used against a dangerous impulse were to fail. The system of projection of evil which Jesus employed was very elaborate, so elaborate in fact, that it leads one to suspect that it may never have been extraordinarily successful. For a year he held out; although once, when the crowd accused him of harboring an unclean spirit, he lost his temper. Then his defence began to fail. He sensed his guilt for the death of the father and felt that he would have to undergo punishment in Jerusalem. At Gethsemane, he made his last stand, projecting his evil onto objects closer and closer to himself. Previously, he had accused only Satan and hypocritical people of evil, but suddenly he began to attack Peter and to teeter on the brink of doubting God. Only one road was open: he would have to undergo punishment, the punishment of death, the death he would have wished upon his father.

The roles which Jesus played, the Suffering Servant and the Son of God, were foreshadowed in the Old Testament; but only Jesus, under the pressure of personal conflict, synthesized the two. We can understand, now, why his disciples should have seen in his life a universal significance: we are all sons of God, in a sense, and we are all murderers. Thus we can explain the impression Jesus has made upon religion: he has acted out one of the essential conflicts of man, the guilt of the son who would kill the father.

NOTES TO CHAPTER I

1. Edward Langton, *Essentials of Demonology* (London, 1949), 66-7; cf. *Vendidad,* xix, 1-7.

2. *The Apocrypha,* trans. E. Goodspeed (New York, 1959), 121.

3. Selby McCasland, *By the Finger of God* (New York, 1951), 66.

4. Langton, *op. cit.,* 81-2.

5. Sigmund Freud, *Totem and Taboo* (New York, 1938), 854.

6. *Ibid.,* 856.

7. Sigmund Freud, *"A Neurosis of Demoniacal Possession in the Seventeenth Century,"* in Collected Papers (London, 1925), IV, 437.

8. Erik H. Erikson, *Childhood and Society* (New York, 1950), 221.

9. Anna Freud, *The Ego and Mechanisms of Defense* (New York, 1946), 132-3.

10. Otto Fenichel, *The Psychoanalytic Theory of Neurosis* (New York, 1945), 41-2.

11. Erikson, *op. cit.,* 224.

12. Fenichel, *op. cit.,* 20.

II

A Forgotten Ecumenist Marriage:
the Puritan and the Jew

1. *Puritan Eschatology in England During the Interregnum*

What is most striking about the progress of eschatological thinking in England during the period of the Civil Wars is the almost total lack of any kind of organized direction with regard to the methods employed to chronicle the growth and decay of history. But however much they may have differed among themselves, the radical sectaries held this view in common: that the expression of authority concentrated in the medieval Papacy had abused its position and in various ways had altered the original commission of the apostolic Church. The commission had been mishandled by what Milton called "a wicked race of deceivers," and by what the Anglican Articles called "the corrupt following of the Apostles." The sectaries therefore claimed the right to turn back to what was to be found in the Old Testament and the New Testament; for them, authority was scriptural, and tradition, however venerable, could be disregarded.

Chronologically, the progress of eschatological thinking in England during the period of the Civil Wars may conveniently be divided into three periods: the first, from 1637 to 1649 when, as a consequence of the National Covenant, the idea of Heaven ceased to be eschatologically oriented in the true sense of the term. The Covenant, which fixed in popular language the prophetic substitution of Scotland for ancient Israel as God's elect and covenanted kingdom, became a Reality in the present, and an inward and outward way of reacting to the world; the second, from 1649 to 1653, when serious Puritan eschatologists completely rejected

the traditional idea of the historical Church as a supernatural and
authoritative instrument for salvation and began to yearn for the
"restoration" of Old Sion's antitype, the apostolic *regnum Christi.*
After the death of Charles in 1649, this was the restoration about
which the words on the new Great Seal of the English Parliament
proclaimed, "In the first year of freedom by God's blessing
restored"; and the third, beginning roughly about the dissolution
of the Barebone's Parliament and the inauguration of Cromwell's
Protectorate in 1653, when radical eschatologists began to empha-
size the recovery of the past by employing both the Deuteronomic
and Levitical Law of Old Testament Israel as their normative
models. Concepts governing the first period still lingered on well
into the second since it was the judgment of radical Puritans, who
urged the conditions of a divine and absolute covenant on England,
that a political counterpart to the covenant of grace was insufficient
to unify all Christians in England in a united and covenanted
front. It was only after 1649, after the "Beast" had been
punished, that a truly popular conviction that Sion could replace
what hitherto had served as a substitute became apparent.

Forced to evoke some kind of heroic age for the launching of
their new visions of the *telos,* to become frontiersmen at a time
when the era of new spiritual frontiers in Reformation England
was already drawing to a close, the radical eschatologists plunged
themselves into the past. It is of course for this reason that the
form of both eschatological prose and poetry of this period was
historical; but it was also a literature with an argument. And in any
literature whose historical sweep is so wide there is room for the
argument to turn in almost any direction that the author wishes.
And, it is equally possible for another, crossing the same ground,
to give the argument at many points quite a different turn.

It requires a high degree of abstraction and generalization to
discover a single cause underlying this new solicitude toward
Scripture as an instrument to chronicle the whole of redemptive
time. Any modern historian who clings to a seventeenth-century
perspective, giving to events or situations which then seemed
important—but left little or no visible trace behind them—the same
weight as to phenomena whose influence dominated a whole
subsequent historical period, seems to deprive himself of the capacity to achieve any real insight into the real significance of his

subject. To claim, for example, that the history of radical Puritan eschatology may be solely in terms of the political history of the Protectorate and the hegemony that ended when Cromwell's control ended, is an argument calculated to appeal to a vestal virgin after being raped by a vandal.

It need hardly be said that such a view loses in depth what it gains in clarity. It muffles the sharp divergence of outlook and interest between those who were united, for widely different reasons, in their hostility to the Orthodox Church; it tends to personify the prophetic role of Cromwell to an extent which, though formally justified by contemporary polemic, masks the power and tenacity of the forces behind him. Sometimes it leads to explanations partial enough to be seriously misleading.

It seems to me that it is logical to begin with a re-examination of causality, or perhaps I should say with the substitution of causal explanation for causality. Not everyone accepts this view. Many may, indeed, feel as Marvell did of the Civil Wars, that "the cause was too good to be fought for"; a thought which has, in the last analysis, all the elusiveness of existentialist metaphysics. First of all, to see those Christians who looked, in an immediate and physical sense, to the Parousia, in seventeenth-century England in terms of strict analogy with those historians who think of time in terms of progress and a permanent change for the better is a habit of long ancestry, going back at least to Plato. This anthropomorphic fallacy—for fallacy it is—is particularly common among those who fail to recognize two fundamental differences between seventeenth-century radical Puritan eschatologists and "progressivist" historians of the past. In the first place, the Puritan sectary is not a pessimist like Philo or Jerome, who diagnoses the basic human malaise in man himself, in an eternal condition whose heavy burden the fathers can never lighten for the sons; and from this flow the second difference, that the Puritan's position *a priori,* is right, from which it follows that disbelief is wrong.

Because of this, some modern rationalists who think that all the Puritan's conceptions and errors may be traced back to the calamitous error in his fundamental conception of God view the radical sectary as a rationalist *malgré lui.* It is suggested that this belief is mainly due to the fact that the rationalist views Puritanism as a whole phenomenologically rather than existentially.

Puritan eschatology is neither biblical, sacramental, historical, nor conciliar theology. Further, it is not Christian theology expounded in terms of any widely accepted philosophy of being. With regard either to the pseudonymic character of the Puritan notions of apocalyptic or to the psychology of the chiliasts themselves, Puritan eschatology is not even a reasoned exposition of ontology. For ontology to be an effective instrument for analyzing existence, it must be closely reasoned. Ontology is, in fact, an attempt to integrate human experience by human reason in proven propositions. The eschatological concepts of the Puritan sectaries, however, proceed from a vision of the universe and of life, unproven and undefended, stated and reiterated with growing emphasis in a semiprophetic manner. All that is essential to Christian history the Puritan eschatologist had reduced to symbols.

One reason why that powerful pair of rationalists' scissors, Cause and Effect, have failed, at least until now, to snip out their patterns in the Puritan vision of time, may lie in the fact that the rendering of Puritan historiographic truths is itself an hypostatized activity, involving the solemn participation of paradigms of persons, and paradigms of myths. We notice, for example, that many Puritans distinguish between myths that function as "local" or personal charters for man or groups of "separated" men to rule certain territories so long as they placate the God, and myths that are held to be mainly national charters, laying claim to the English Canaan, to the New Jerusalem, and to the status of the chosen people of God. The demonstration of the alleged characteristics of these myths by the mythographer, however, suffers from a number of defects deriving ultimately from the piecemeal nature of the argument and from the neglect of analytical ideas about the collective presentations which can be, or were, useful.

The fundamentalist *malleus maleficarum* who subscribes to the first myth, is a Puritan whose vision of God far more nearly approaches the Absolute of Hegel—that is, of a universal "oneness in diversity of being," pursued, of course, by dialectic—than the Puritan who urges the myth of the Elect Nation. The first Puritan is not merely engaged in marketing old goods under a new name. He is engaged in a moving and concrete dialectic, the numerous variations and derivatives of which do not immediately seem to offer us a paradigm of things or of the laws of things.

Rather, it seems to offer a simplified dramatic picture of the process by which an individual mind, torn between inadequate and apparently contradictory abstractions, between polarities, creates for itself a richly concrete but precariously stable universe. But once we spot the Baconian perversity of this dialectic whereby a universal truth is symbolized (mythologized) in some materialistic notion that was taking shape even as its author wrote, and when we analyze the Puritan myth of personal salvation structurally, without regard to period or to expository variation, in order to expose the dialectic and the values with which it is constantly concerned, we are forced to respond to the challenge of the structuralist principle that holds a myth to consist of all its versions and recognize that each Puritan's individual myth concerning his own personal salvation has a rather adventitious character, appearing to be guided by no clear rule of investigation either of method of analysis or of temporal framework. In other words, a myth resembling Hamlet without the prince.

When we turn to examine the Puritan who lays claim to the myth of corporate salvation, and the charter of Christ's millennial kingdom on earth, one is reminded of de Tocqueville's suggestion that the merits and shortcomings of a government can best be studied by observing its operation in its distant overseas possessions. In developing this theme, this Puritan imposes on himself some rather severe limitations. His starting point is the assertion—not, perhaps, clearly substantiated—that the traditional aims of natural philosophy have become obsolete. Hence the crisis in method and the successive attempts to discover a new basis to undermine the Orthodox view of Christian time.

Perhaps the most fortuitous hit occurred when his thought was still anchored to historical reality. To the question, "Must not a sound philosophy of salvation be based on a scale of being in which the lower forms of life justifiably serve the higher?" he replied in the affirmative. Because of this, he was led, like the Cartesian and the Jansenist, to obliterate all except God. But recognizing that the Neo-Platonic separation of matter and spirit undermined the aims and methods of traditional philosophy, he came to believe that man was an integrated being; spirit, soul, and body formed an organic unit, and all were receptacles of divine grace. Like Gregory Palamus and St. Gregory, he thought all men capable of theosis. For him, salvation for the Elect was like a raft: you never sank, but your feet were never dry.

His liking for theocratic absolutism led him to test the validity of the older Puritan hypothesis that held that the law of nature and the facts of the future could be discovered analytically by *a priori* considerations. It was, in his view, an error, which he denounced with unmistakable clarity. If it had been possible, he would have called in aid Locke's refutation of innate ideas; but he would probably have had a formidable task in disproving Kant's arguments that *synthetic a priori* knowledge was possible.

Yet the attempt to treat all the Puritans' efforts to answer the question of the *a priori* knowledge of natural laws as if they had no ecology produces a sense of strain. It is as if one were to study dancing bees under an arc lamp, and try to work out the meaning of their activities without considering the needs and nature of the hive.

The idea which all Puritans deprecate was fathered by the Pythagoreans, and the Pythagorean belief in the harmony of nature found expression in two great systems, those of Kepler and Descartes. It was to Descartes that the seventeenth century owed the most comprehensive attempt to construct a system of the world on *a priori* principles, but in his day, it swayed all Europe except England. The Puritans, in a strange alliance with the scientific world, sided with a modified Newtonian empiricism, modified in the sense that Newton was not so empirical as he is often represented to be. It is to him that we owe the declaration, *Natura enim simplex est.*

In essence, the Puritan's argument is that older Christian eschatology, if properly understood, contains an ethic and teleology and that, in stressing the "meaninglessness" of human events and institutions, it subtly betrays Christian doctrine. The Puritan, in a sense, joins a Benthamite devotion to method to the notion, derived from continental sources, that there could be a science of last things and first things capable of mapping the path to human perfectibility. But the sheer arbitrariness of such an approach hardly needs illustration: Puritanism plus method plus science can be deadly.

Idealists of that sort may be tempted to regard themselves as heaven-sent saviors of mankind, to brush aside as reactionary the "reasonable" objections of their fellow citizens, to become convinced that their own temperamentally conditioned panaceas are based on scientifically proven laws, and hence to use transcendent means for the achievement of transcendent ends. The Puritans' ambivalent use of the word reason, for example, is employed most disconcertingly to reflect a whole spectrum of differing meanings, now Sir Thomas Browne's "rationall sowle," now consciousness, now purpose, now explosive emotional activity.

Without an inborn affinity, many Puritans argue, few can sail through his myth without a steersman. There is indeed a very fine line between arguing that no tradition is good in itself and arguing that no reasonable criterion of natural law could justify the attempt to transcend it. This is illustrated by the fact that when the Puritan analyzes some central doctrine of the Christian faith, he sometimes strips Christianity of all that cannot be experimentally verified, and at other times remythologizes the Gospel.

It was only by simultaneous examination of the historical and mythological levels of the world that the Puritan could hope to make sense of the entanglement of *dies*; such an examination already required of him a competence in more than one specialized area. He employed the languages of halachic casuistry, of probability theory, of covenant theology. This sounds like, and was, a wide enough range of interacting forces to explain almost anything as now one, now another gains the ascendant; but language notwithstanding, the Puritan's basic theme and his concern was a vision of the future.

Agreeing with Plato that only supra-sensible forms were "objects" of knowledge per se, and with Aristotle that the sphere of knowledge was merely the kind of thing that could not be otherwise, the Puritan took his stand on a metaphysical Indus, convinced that within a short time the world of nature would be subjugated. In other words, forgetfulness of Origen's teaching that scripture was to be understood in several different ways, constituted a rejection of an absolute truth of created nature, that is, a rejection of the existence of a hierarchy of knowledge.

At one end of the scale comes precise scientific knowledge of those features of experience that can be treated as objects which exist independently and distinct from us; at the other end is the knowledge we have of other persons by our involvement with

them, and this is a type of knowledge we can have only when we
stop treating them as objects. This sort of realistic point-of-view is
by no means naive, and in the end it seems almost to disappear
into an unattainable Kantian noumenon.

The Puritan's principal focus with regard to the descriptiveness
of his vision was that scientific explanation demanded that scriptural laws were to be seen as *causal,* not merely as descriptive, and
that the essence of causality lay in the interpretation of changing
phenomena as the manifestations of identities persisting through
time. Hence the Decalogue, Deuteronomic law, and the covenant
of works were in a sense *a priori*, although it could happen that
what was legislated may have been wrongly identified, as when
Descartes postulated a law of conservation of motion, and was
shown by Newton and Leibniz to be mistaken in his definition
of motion.

The Puritan proceeded from this Parmenidean point to the
point where he considered his vision of the end of history as one
manifestation of nature's resistance to the constraints of causality,
a resistance which was ultimately unintelligible. In other words, for
the Puritan eschatologist there is no real identity of cause and
effect, but only the Parmenidean universe of mechanism. He
would probably argue that when we pass from biblical laws to
their causes, we postulate the existence of a material law-giver;
we then must specify the properties that law-giver must possess
in order to fulfill his function of explaining law. The process of
explanation consists in the expression of certain concepts in terms
of others, and an end is reached when we come to what may be
called a general conceptual system, which is a set of ideas regarded as basic and therefore needing no further reduction.
But beyond this point, his argument would not proceed in so
orderly a fashion.

It is one thing to assert axiomatically that words whether
biblical or otherwise—carry meanings which represent images of
objective reality; it is something quite different to assert that words
are or imply "fictions," mythical vestures of truth. In fact, this
distinction makes all the difference. If, in developing a methodology
to approach the question of the *telos* of history, the Puritan had
stopped at the point where he confused scripture with reality, he
would most probably have attempted to make of abstract

formulations an authority greater than the obstinate disorder of history. Indeed, historians might have seen in this use of a concrete empirical praxis for essentially metaphysical ends, signs of a new sort of Puritan root heresy. But the Puritan was not foolish enough to believe that he could instrumentalize words by using them as deeds. That would be in effect to analyze the Old Testament as *Vorständnis* to the Gospel (in the Bultmannian sense).

The Puritan, aware of the fact that he lived intellectually in an untidy universe, expected a certain degree of tension between words and things. Far more significant for his apprehending of the future, he was aware that the recognition of qualities, and species of things that manifest them, was his proper study; also, he suspected that "motions" on the earth and in the heavens could turn out to be indifferent exemplars of the same laws; and so, like Bruno of Nola, he waited for divisions between ideality and reality to be reconciled in heaven.

But if the concordance of opposites is understood more philosophically, as granting—as in an epiphany—insight into reality, then the incidents and events pointing to the concordance may be viewed existentially in a far-reaching historical process and can be understood only in the light of that process. In other words, immanental and transcendental elements enter into the Puritan's concept of historical change. In history, he found a terrain where the mystery which condescends to human experience could be reconciled with the mystery which transcends it.

In this attitude, the Puritan is linked both by his semantic affiliations to a conception of the present as actual and the past as symbolical, and to an affirmation of the permanency of man; and in terms of imagery, he is also linked to symbol-objects such as time, matter and knowledge. He distinguished between two types of knowledge; the first of which may be termed the horizontal, where the intelligence is on the same level as the object of knowing, and the second of which may be termed the vertical, where it is not. In the one case, the intelligence is sought, in the other it is initiated. In other words, the mythology of materialism functioned, for the Puritan, as an ersatz of reality in much the same way as the mythology of surrealism functioned as an ersatz transcendence.

For example, he thought that the greatest discoveries always abstract from picturable models: if it were ever possible to represent completely the structure of eschatological theory, this would consist entirely of an empirical axiom system, concentrated, foreshortened, symbolized. In this context, one of his chief methodological paradoxes was that scripture worked by playing on what may be termed stock responses (proto-logical and logical thoughts); he believed that the received symbols, the analogies, the types and antitypes, were the right ones. Since he believed that until the pragmatic test was applied by Christ at his Parousia, this belief that Scripture was a masterpiece of empirical knowledge was extraordinarily easy to support.

And like the shamans described by Eliade, the Puritan often acted as diviner and prophet as well as theological linguist; but his language was not an organism; it was a system of notation, which was often used to expound or solve a specific moral problem, or, reaching beyond the knowledge of human experience and understanding, to "show" what could not be logically said. The inorganic nature of his language was illustrated by his determination to give every action (even the sounding of a trumpet) its maximum transcendent significance. In addition, the Puritan did not seem to appreciate how difficult it could be to translate theological knowledge into action.

To some this might seem explaining *obscurum per obscurius,* associating it with David's sin of numbering the people. But when we recognize that the Puritan believed the methods of empiricism truly applicable to theological issues, the relationship between his language and reality becomes a bit clearer: his was an onlooker's language, and he himself an onlooker with an object.

It is the disintegration of form which distinguishes his language when the Puritan addressed himself to that most fundamental of all questions, is God real? If God is the *ens realissimum,* the Being most real, the debate cannot be conducted at the merely verbal level. Since the Puritan realized that God is not objective in the sense in which science commonly understands objectivity—he is not, for example, a "God of the gaps"—he was led to analyze the subjective issue of the covenant relationship between God and man. This caused him to declare, in effect, that belief in God's existence is inescapably metaphysical because it is his belief about what is real in itself; and he found a necessary connection between belief and worship, which is, in terms of covenant relationships, a response of love and gratitude based on the recognition of an ultimate reality which is itself loving and trustworthy. In terms of reformation doctrine, this is a more orthodox conclusion, in a sense, than that of Calvin or Bucer, who, while satisfied that science had not destroyed the case for belief, held that just what practical expression could be given to faith still remained to be worked out.

These ideas were necessarily fundamental, though differing, as all of the Puritan's did, according to a symbolic or an epistemological emphasis. But he believed that if an observer looked to these principles, he would naturally find in them an expression of their cosmogony. The trouble with this *ex cathedra* assertion is not that it completely lacks truth, but that it is so partial a statement of the truth that it would require a volume to set it into proper context.

In one sense, the Puritan is safe from being reproached with logic, Cartesian or otherwise. When, for example, he inveighed against those who wished to sweep primitivistic symbols pointing to a foreshortened eschatology under the mat with Cartesian logic, the Puritan did not argue that all history was a seamless web and that there were no real discontinuities; rather he claimed that a strong continuity existed between the past, the future, and the institutions he was working to erect in the present. Indeed, the Puritan's "primitivism," because it related to his belief that the norm was the past, exalted both chronological and cultural symbols. The Hebraic past and its covenantal institutions were exalted. Further, rejecting Oresian historiography which projected a pattern of progressive development of Christian history, the Puritan's hope for the future was eschatological in a new way: the *telos* of history was viewed as if it were a symbolic restitution of the past.

This is a partial explanation of why Puritan eschatologists worshipped rather than not; theirs was a theology that looked to stability and achievement rather than to perpetual change; that respected halachic concepts of covenant obligation rather than rejected them; theirs was a projected society that was hierarchical, and was everywhere outwardly symbolical of its inward values; a society in which the covenanters were visibly covenanted, the prophets prophetic, and the separatists separated. The Puritan has a generalized nostalgic vision of this sort of theology and this sort of society as essentially one; and the unavoidable knowledge that whenever it had existed, it had disappeared in a *triplex discessio*.

The Puritan discussion of the future is so largely taken up with the allegorical illumination of history through a study of the semantic questions of periodicity, *termini ad quem et a quo*, that it seems as if the issue of what kind of historical restitution they want is forgotten. Indeed, some modern observers claim that the intelligence that orders their thinking, acute and confident though it is, functions very much like the Medusa's head—it petrifies what it fixes on.

His observations about history, in other words, reveal a Ptolemaic fallacy of supposing that the historical point from which he focuses is not subject to the same kind of laws as the phenomena observed. Because of this, it is not too misleading to conceive of the Puritan as an existential counterfeiter. When he studies the meaning of history, he is looking not so much for a world view as for an escape route of his own along the lines of covenant goals in their widest and deepest meanings. History's meaning could be grasped by a study of the covenant's origin, progressive unfolding, and culmination. His process of assimilating history then, was also a process of transformation. It was carried out in opposition to historical fact, and the strength of the opposition depends on the strength of the covenant's initial influence: his process of assimilating history, therefore, was a gigantic *reductio ad absurdum* rather than a blueprint for the future.

If irony is the right word for all this, it is surely even more ironic that covenant theology was the instrument whereby history and revelation could coalesce with reason. This is a difficulty endemic in his Socratic approach to covenants, in the detachment that insists on rationalizing intuitions, and he ends up discussing the highly ideological question: "are all the senses of *regnum Christi* compatible in time?" with a remarkable freedom from ideology.

The Puritan revolution failed to agree upon the meaning of the Kingdom of Christ. One group of Puritans viewed the Kingdom of Christ montanistically as a weapon both to undermine the dogmatic and secularized structure of orthodox Christianity, and to illustrate the universality of the moral and ethical code contained in the Hebraic covenant of works. Another group used *regnum Christi* chiefly as a metaphorical cannister which, preparing for the eschatological drama, pointed prophetically to a future historical reality. A third group of Puritans, in their Donatist emphasis upon separation, viewed the Kingdom of Christ within a context, which, when they insisted upon a thorough reformation of Church and State modeled after the Pristine purity of the Apostolic Church, assumed a revolutionary urgency.

Puritans, then, departed from Augustine's concept of the *regnum Christi* as the visible, terrestrial church; and though all methodologically applied the balm of synchronizing ancient history with biblical chronology to the wounds of redemptive time, they uniformly saw in the flow of time signs pointing neither to degeneration in St. Cyprian's sense nor signs pointing to progress and perfectibility in the Joachimite sense, but rather, as I have suggested earlier, signs looking forward to a primitivistic restitution of the past, signs which would precede the days of the Lord. Further, unlike Luther or Calvin, the radical Puritan's vision of the future was neither an eschatology of degeneration and collapse nor an eschatology of progressivism; despite his attempt to bring down from heaven a theocracy, the *regnum Christi* could not, for him, be perfected on earth.

2. *Philosemitism and Jewish Resettlement in England*

In the year 1290, King Edward I decreed the expulsion of all Jews then living in England. Some 16,000 departed in the summer of that year, and England was to see no more of them—in theory at least—until Oliver Cromwell permitted their unobtrusive return three and a half centuries later.

During the intervening centuries, a number of Jews did in fact reside in London, even worshipping at a clandestine synagogue in St. Catherine's parish. Although their presence was known to parishioners and civil authority alike, it was little heeded. Indeed, it may be presumed that they very likely comprised the more desirable social element of that parish, which had acquired the character of a haven for aliens, assorted heretics, and unfrocked priests. One of their number, Don Antonio Carvajal, was even known to exert some influence with Edward Nicholas, Charles I's Secretary of State.[1]

In the year 1655, a rabbi from Amsterdam, Menasseh ben Israel, received the Protector's permission to visit England and petition Parliament to lift the ban on Jewish immigration. Menasseh arrived and addressed a committee assembled at Whitehall, composed of government officials, lawyers, prominent theologians, and merchants. This body proved more hostile than had been expected and, despite Cromwell's efforts to the contrary, denied Menasseh's request. The form taken by their opposition, however, was not to deny admission outright, but rather to restrict the terms of admission, i.e., the limitations which were to be imposed on the new residents. After a fortnight of unproductive debate, Cromwell dismissed the committee and pursued an independent course of action. During the remainder of his rule, he quietly allowed some Jews to settle in England extra-legally, a policy later continued by Charles II. As Heinrich Graetz states, "The Jews were not admitted in triumph through the great portal, but . . . let in by Cromwell through a back door."[2]

But whatever the manner of the Jews' entrance, it was not by chance that the revolutionary years marked the beginning of their recall to England. Several developments favorable to the Jews had recently occurred. For one thing, principles of toleration had become widespread, and embraced the Jews along with dissident Protestant sectarians. Indeed, the equating of Jews with Christian sectaries was possible, among other reasons, because one of the most striking phenomena of the time had evoked new behavioral similarities: their common expectation of the imminent arrival of the Messiah.[3] Moreover, while the Kingdom of God in England seemed imminent to many of the Protestant sects, Christian theology had traditionally held that this Kingdom could be fulfilled only after the conversion of the Jews, and only after the Jews had been scattered throughout the four quarters of the world; both conditions, it was obvious, to many Puritans, would not be possible without Jewish readmission into England.[4] To delay readmission to the Jews would in effect be to delay the arrival of the Messiah.

Economic motives, on the other hand, were not absent from the discussion, and to be sure, played a dominant part in Cromwell's thought: England, it was argued, might learn from those countries on the continent (particularly the Dutch Republic) to whose economies the Jews were making substantial contributions.[5] Most crucial, however, was the regard in which Puritanism held the Old Testament—a regard whose purview was ultimately enlarged to include the "people of" that book. It was primarily certain Puritan affinities with the Old Testament that conditioned the forms in which philosemitism expressed itself.

In general, all but the most extreme of the Protestant sects who took part in the Republican upheaval (such as the Antinomians) sought and found guidance in the pages of the Old Testament rather than those of the New. A rationality that could be found in the Hebraic conceptions of justice, and a will to social reform that could be discerned in the prophetic books, were used as paradigms for the Puritans' own historical situation. The chaos of the times even moved some extremists to bridge the gaps of space and time, and seek to base the social order directly on the Deuteronomic and Levitical laws of the Old Testament.

It was the "rationality" of the Old Testament that was of primary importance for the English Calvinists, for it was they who acquired the political power taken from the King. Although Calvin had at first taught that good works counted for nought in the pursuit of salvation, he later made work an important constituent of his religious doctrine. The ambiguity of the Calvinistic idea of work has never been resolved within the realm of theology alone, and may perhaps be best understood psychologically. If a devotee truly believed that his destiny was foreordained, then he might have concluded logically that moral behavior (i.e., good works) did not need to concern him. Justification by good works, however, entered Calvinism not through theological necessity but through psychological need—specifically, man's longing to ascertain his soul's ultimate destiny. The doctrine of predestination, it might be added, divided its adherent into two selves, one whose damnation or salvation was already concluded, and a second whose purpose it was to ferret out the conclusion. It was the second who carried on the business of living, seeking constantly to elicit hints from his companion-self as to what the fate of the both of them was likely to be. The Puritan was obliged to be objective; he had always had to scrutinize his own nature and his binary self. His problem, however, was that his utterly sinful nature was untrustworthy, so he felt, to provide information on which the objective self might rely. Might not a wicked nature deliberately falsify, or even mislead the objective self? Deeds, on the other hand, were made of more solid stuff.

Inevitably, a certain tension had to exist between the two selves. Natural behavior was bound to be sinful and had to be checked by reason. This process, predicated as it was upon the constancy of human nature, was carried to its logical conclusion of equally constant self-criticism and self-abasement. The Puritan was his own stern and implacable judge. But this was not for him merely a process of occasional purging by introspection; it was not occasional but continuous; not purgative—as in psychoanalysis —but retributive. Sins might not be forgiven, only accumulated. Thus the God of the Puritans was not one upon whom the believer might call for comfort, for He was as infinitely great as man was infinitesimally small. For the Puritan, God acted "according to the unsearchable council of His own will, whereby He extendeth, or with-holdeth mercy, as He pleaseth, for the glory of His sovereign power over His creatures, to pass by, and to ordain them to dishonour and wrath for their sin, to the praise of His glorious justice."[6]

For the Catholic, a sacramental "magic" might reconcile the two selves, dispel the tension that had arisen between them.[7] The Calvinist, however, could resolve his inner tension only through labor, activity, and through what Max Weber called "worldly asceticism." Labor, the pursuit of a calling, displaced onto the external world the tension which the Puritan had turned inward. He set reason to work ordering what he found in his environment.

Into what form should the environment be modeled? Whatever form seemed to indicate "the greater glory of God," he answered. The Old Testament indicated certain forms which had once been very pleasing to God. Here was the grounding for the Puritan rationality: the Old Testament gave the Puritan both a set of divinely sanctioned ends and a strategy of means. The detailed program of ethical action and behavior elucidated in the Mosaic Code of 613 Commandments expressed a spirit with which he might identify himself—an identification which he attempted in its form if not always in its details.

If he were indeed one of the Elect of God, a true instrument of the Divine Will, he might expect success in his enterprises, for success was not a mere reward for virtuous deeds, but a consequence of virtuous being. The measure of success was taken, as Weber says, "in private profitableness." "For if that God, whose hand the Puritan sees in all the occurrences of life, shows one of His elect a chance of profit, He must do it with a purpose . . . the faithful Christian must follow the call by taking advantage of the opportunity."[8] Reward, for the Puritan, then, was consistent with virtue, although not necessarily caused by it. This distinction was subtle and susceptible of neglect in daily affairs, however. And although ambiguous, as Weber has shown, the causal link between virtue and reward often insinuated itself into practical life.

Evidence corroborating this relationship was not lacking in the Old Testament: "The righteous eateth to the satisfying of his soul: but the belly of the wicked shall want," instructed the Book of Proverbs (13.25). God might well have addressed the seventeenth-century English Calvinists as He had the nation of Israel upon presenting them with the Decalogue: "Ye shall walk in all the ways which the Lord your God hath commanded you, that ye may live, and that it may be well with you, and that ye may prolong your days in the land which ye shall possess" (Deuteronomy 5.33). Moreover, the entire twenty-eighth chapter of Deuteronomy listed the temporal rewards that would follow on adherence to the Law, in addition to the temporal punishments that would follow transgression.

The Book of Judges provided a like paradigm even on the level of a nation. It was read as the cycle of punishment and reward of an alternately faithless and repentant Jewish nation. When the nation had erred severely, foreign conquerors had descended to execute the Lord's wrath; its return to righteousness then induced the Lord to raise up a Judge, like Deborah or Gideon, who had turned out the conquerors and restored peace and piety to Israel.

Such a rationale was not a monopoly of the Puritan sects. The Baptists, too, found it useful in solving certain spiritual problems. According to Baptist doctrine, God's grace descended upon any individual who was willing and prepared to receive it by a voluntary commitment of will, and election was confirmed by the individual's own intuition. Such a doctrine, however, could

quickly lead to the position of the Antinomians, for whom the
state of grace, being completely subjective and personal, signified the end of all forms of objective law and social order. To
forestall Antinomian conclusions, some Baptist writers held (as
had Luther) that grace was a precarious state, one which had
constantly to be renewed; others, that the initial attainment of
grace was only a beginning, the first step in a striving for ever
higher degrees of spiritual perfection. At all events, it was necessary to have some yardstick, some objective proof of the state of
grace. Voluntary, committed, and continuous imitation of the
actions of the righteous men in the Scriptures proved admirably
suited to such a purpose. But while the New Testament could
provide only general attitudes, the Old Testament offered a
specific, concrete program for life.[9]

Among the Quakers, a certain minority carried the updating
process to extremes. George Fox, founder of the sect, reported
that many of his disciples, especially the females, taking Isaiah
20.2-3 as their text,[10] walked naked and barefoot through
certain villages as a sign of their forthcoming destruction. One
"Solomon Eccles" (the surname is an abbreviation of Ecclesiastes;
Solomon, the supposed author of the book) strolled through
Smithfield with a "pan of fire and supposed brimstone on his
head" and only a cloth around his waist proclaiming the invidious
comparison between the city and Biblical Sodom.[11] Among
the Rosicrucians—to whom their present namesakes bear little
resemblance—a physician, Robert Fludd, published in 1659 the
Mosaical Philosophy, in which he endeavored to derive a cosmology by mystical interpretation of the Mosaic law.[12]

The Puritan Revolution with considerable vigor injected
into England the will to social justice, and for much of it the
vehicle was the Old Testament. The political tyranny of both
King and Parliament, the abuse of economic power by large land-
owners, the maladministration of justice, the persecution of religious minorities—against such social evils were the Puritan reformers able to invoke Scriptural texts. Many, indeed, considered
themselves in the tradition of Biblical heroes, agents on earth of
Heaven's will.

Most popular among the Puritans were the prophetic books—
Joshua, Judges, Samuel and Kings.[13] Their message was

essentially that man had it in his power to order the world justly if he would but seek God's way to accomplish it. Oliver Cromwell, flying a banner proclaiming himself the "Lion of Judah,"[14] would often shout some Old Testament text as he rode into battle.[15] His inspired Hebraicism extended even to his army's password, which is reported to have been "The Lord of Hosts."[16] The judges Gideon and Judah Maccabee were the heroes to whom Cromwell often compared himself, for like himself, Gideon had hesitated before accepting the Lord's charge, and the Maccabees, whose small force defeated the more numerous Greeks, were said to have fought with "sword in hand, and praise of God in their mouth."[17] Often, another sect of radical Puritans known as the Levellers styled themselves Jews and their enemies Amalekites, or called the royal house of Stuart "the Egyptian bondage"; and John Lilburne, one of their leaders, described by George Sabine as "a master of popular agitation with a genius for dramatizing himself before the public as the embodiment of the people's liberties,"[18] compared himself to youthful David, the slayer of giants. The prevalence of Old Testament names such as Abigail, Abner, Praise-God, etc. is so familiar it requires no further elaboration.

With effective influence far greater than their small numbers bespoke—there were never more than fifty or sixty—the Diggers too sounded the call for reform. Their leader, Gerard Winstanley, differed somewhat from other reformers in the method with which he employed the Scriptural model. True beliefs, Winstanley asserted, necessarily originate in the heart, but require corroboration in the history of real experience which Scriptural truth appropriately provides.[19] Like all reformers from the Presbyterians leftward, the Diggers railed particularly against prelates and lawyers alike, who made God and Divine justice inaccessible, and in addition extracted titles and exorbitant fees.

Another favorite bogey of the Puritan revolution was the Normans: Winstanley, for example, inveighs against lawyers for keeping the law in Latin and French as well as for their fees. Comparing Joshua to William the Conqueror, he contrasts the former's policy of dividing the land of Canaan equitably among the tribes with the latter's unenlightened distribution of land to servants and friend.[20] Moreover, he predicted that God would "make the

barren land fruitful" and "remove the Egyptian bondage of the
Normans." In many similar quotations, he repeats the theme of
weakness embattled against strength, and good against evil:
Israel and Midian, Moses and Pharaoh, Jacob and Esau. His
favorite prophetic sources are Amos, Micah, Jeremiah, and
Hosea, all of which are replete with the spirit of social justice and
humanitarianism.

In Hosea 4.1-2, for instance, God proclaims a controversy with
Israel, for ". . . there is no truth, nor mercy, nor knowledge of
God in the land. By swearing, and lying, and killing, and stealing,
and committing adultery, they break out, and blood toucheth
blood." The Lord, in Micah 3.1-4, chastens the tyrant in
strong and emotional language: "Hear . . . O heads of Jacob,
and ye princes of the house of Israel; is it for you to know judgment! Who hate the good and love the evil; who pluck off their
skin from them, and their flesh from oft their bones . . . they shall
cry unto the Lord, but he will not hear them: he will even hide his
face from them at that time, as they have behaved themselves ill
in their doings." Israel will be severely punished, declares the Lord
in Amos 5.12: "For I know your manifold transgressions and
your mighty sins: they afflict the just, they take a bribe, and they
turn aside the poor in the gate. . . ."

John Lilburne, the Leveller leader, drew upon Proverbs
21.13 for the title of his book *The Poore Man's Cry*: "Whoso
stoppeth his ears at the cry of the poor, he also shall cry himself but
shall not be heard" but he might also have turned to 14.31 of the
same book: "He that oppresseth the poor reproacheth his Maker,
but he that honoureth him hath mercy on the poor." Like Cromwell
and others, Lilburne considered himself in part an instrument to
effect God's will on earth. The analogy with David, which he
himself affirmed, has already been cited; but he also considered
himself, as did the Biblical prophets, an instrument to make
known that same will. His companions likened him to Jeremiah,
and indeed, Lilburne's mission was more comparable to the ethical
mission of the prophet from Anatoth than to the predominantly
military one of King David. He was provoked by the same un-
yielding forces that impelled Jeremiah (20.9): "His word was in
my heart as a burning fire shut up in my bones, and I was weary
with forbearing, and I could not stay." In fine, as D. B. Robertson

has correctly written, all the Levellers felt themselves "within the framework of Biblical prophetic thinking."[21]

During the turbulent middle decades of the seventeenth century in England, institutions replaced each other with incredible rapidity. After having cast out Crown and Old Priest, the Long Parliament and its New Presbyters were themselves turned out by the New Model Army under Cromwell. Under the army's aegis, they were followed shortly by the Rump Parliament, whose decree brought Charles I to the scaffold in 1649, and later by the Barebone's "Parliament of Saints," in 1653. In 1659, the shaky Protectorate of Richard Cromwell, which his father Oliver, the Lord Protector, had sustained through the support of the army, collapsed when the cohesion of the army was shattered. A resurrected Rump Parliament restored the Monarchy of the Stuart house, and with it Episcopacy, and then dissolved the army itself. The old notions of authority were challenged, and something was needed to take their place, something which could stand permanent and impregnable when the traditional rules of religion and politics were in flux. Lilburne and his fellow Leveller Richard Overton wrote in 1647 that the net effect of the Presbyterian revolution was to "Dissolve the legall frame and constitution of the civill policy and government of the Kingdome, by suffering will and lies, but not law to rule and governe us, and so reduce us into the originall Law of nature, for every man to preserve and defend himselfe the best he can."[22] At such times do men turn to the laws and traditions of the "golden ages" of their history. Thus did God's designated of seventeenth-century England turn to the Law of the Old Testament, whose observance had made the Israelite nation holy.

This Hebraicizing tendency was especially strong among the Baptist sectaries. Since the acquiring of God's grace depended largely on man's obedience of revealed law, it was quite natural for pious men to equate the precepts of positive law with those of revealed law, in order that no man-made barriers might be interposed between themselves and God.[23] Thus, for example, Winstanley looked forward to a time when each man could be his own intercessor before God and the law. In *The Law of Freedom* (1652), Winstanley entitles Chapter two "The King's Old Laws Cannot Govern a Free Commonwealth," and reasons that "They cannot govern in time of bondage, and in times of freedom too: they have indeed served many masters, Popish and Protestant." He proposed a "commonwealth" constructed on a communist legal framework, and argued that "While Israel was under this Commonwealth Government, they were a terror to all oppressing Kings . . . and so will England be, if this righteous Law become our Governor. . . ." In *Regall Tyrannie*, a treatise attributed to Lilburne, the author avers that people should have a voice in choosing rulers, since even God, in appointing Saul, David, and Solomon as Kings of Israel, "would not impose them upon the people of Israel against their own wills. . . ."[24]

Veneration of Deuteronomic and Levitical Law reached its zenith in 1653, when many members of Barebone's Parliament were not only prepared to lift its statutes directly out of the Old Testament and impose them as law upon contemporaries, but in fact accomplished just that. Approximately thirty of the 140 Parliamentarians were members of the radical millenarian group called the "Fifth Monarchy Men," and another thirty were of various Baptist persuasions, with whom they often cooperated. Although unable by themselves to enact legislation, they were successfully able to obstruct what they wished.[25] Major-General Thomas Harrison, the sometime fanatic leader of the Fifth Monarchists, advocated immediate adoption of Levitical government. He also proposed a state council patterned after the Sanhedrinnic judiciary of the Second Jewish Commonwealth. William Aspinall, a chiliast and messianist like Harrison, maintained that the only valid laws were those of the Bible, and envisaged a stratum of "Divines" and "Saints" who, together with deputies of their appointment, would govern with absolute power.[26] But saintliness was found unsuited to the necessarily sinful task of governance, and the saints were replaced by the Protectorate within several months.

During this period, the double-edged sword of textual interpretation was wielded with equal facility by separatists and non-separatists, monarchists and anti-monarchists, proponents and opponents of religious toleration. "Distortion!" was the usual hue and cry raised by antagonists. The prolonged and heated battle over words led Rufus Jones to call English Puritanism during the revolutionary period a "forensic" religious system,[27] with the formal resolution being the whole of the Scriptures, from "In the beginning" to the very end of Chronicles. John Sadler, in *Rights of the Kingdom* (1649), for example, advanced the republican principle of the crown's subordination to the divinely-sanctioned law of Scripture by seeking to show that this principle was obtained and applied to ancient Judea.[28] At the same time, it was argued by others—who did not accept Lilburne's ingenious assumptions[29] —that the kings of Israel had been appointed with, and ruled by, divine consent, and consequently that they commanded absolute obedience of its subjects. Theocratic proponents of state-imposed obedience to religion could cite God's injunction to Israel in Exodus 23 to drive out the Canaanites "lest they make thee sin against Me," while dissenters turned to Genesis 13, in which Abraham was permitted by the Canaanites to dwell among them undisturbed. In *The ancient bounds, or liberty of conscience tenderly stated* . . . (1645), Francis Rous, member of Parliament and later a delegate to the Whitehall Conference, argued that the antagonists of religious toleration who drew on Old Testament texts for support were guilty of grave misinterpretation. To be sure, he went on to correct their errors.[30]

Great popular unrest, which grew steadily under the first two Stuarts and erupted into bloody warfare during the Interregnum and Protectorate, spawned innumerable sects. Prior to 1641, or the beginning of the Long Parliament, all faiths except that of the Established Episcopal Church were repressed with a severity that was greatest under Archbishop Laud. It was in this period of Stuart rule that persecution (among other factors) prompted the *Mayflower* expedition in 1620, and the flight to the New World of approximately 25,000 people in the decade before 1640. Sects crystallized around any crude particle of religious novelty or doctrinal ball of strife that chance presented. Only through mutual toleration could a *modus vivendi,* an uneasy co-existence, be possible. As Leonard Busher wrote in *Religious Peace* (1614), one of the earliest pleas in England for universal religious toleration and liberty of conscience, ". . . If the believing should persecute the unbelieving to death, who should remain alive?" [31]

Those who had expected more enlightened behavior from the Presbyterian Long Parliament were disappointed, however. Especially was this true of Cromwell and his band of "Ironsides,"

composed mainly of Sectaries, who had, by its large contribution
to the defeat of the King and his Cavaliers, placed the sceptre
in the hands of that body. In 1648, Colonel Pride and his men
purged the Parliament of members hostile to themselves. From
then until his death in 1658, it was Cromwell, backed by the
army, who controlled English policy at home and abroad. Needless
to say, his policy was, in general, one of moderate toleration. There
was, however, one group of whom the protective cover of
toleration did not reach—the group constituted by the Catholics;
in addition, the Anglicans, to some extent still operative as a
cohesive unit, were also occasionally expelled from underneath it.
The Jews, on the other hand, were often mentioned as a particular
object of toleration. Even more important, the regimen of tolerance
allowed, and even encouraged to some degree, the free activity of
sects which, in various degrees and at various times, favored
the Jews, some of whose activities and dispositions have already
been mentioned.

The most obviously and monolithically philosemitic sectaries
were the "Fifth-Monarchy Men." Basing their beliefs mainly
on Chapter 7 of the book of Daniel, they considered the reign
of the Kingdom of God, i.e., "the Fifth Monarchy," near at hand.
The first four had been the Assyrian, Persian, Greek, and Roman.
Observing a great decline in the power of the Holy Roman Empire
in the last years of the Thirty Years' War, many of these radical
sectaries sensed the end of the fourth monarchy and the imminence
of a new age which would usher in the millennial Kingdom of God
on earth. The more republican in sentiment, of course, interpreted
Charles' fall (his corresponding Scriptural type was usually understood to be the little horn in Daniel's vision) and Cromwell's
establishment as the fulfillment of this Scriptural prophecy.[32]

When these millennial calculators learned, in 1652, of
Cromwell's intentions to establish a government of holy men, and
an "Assembly of Divines" later known collectively as Barebone's
Parliament, they hailed him "as the Moses who was to establish
the new order, the chief ruler appointed by God."[33] Opening
the short career of this body on July 4, 1653, Cromwell responded
in kind by declaring: "I say, you are called with a high call. . . .
We are at the threshold, and therefore it becomes us to lift up our
heads and to encourage ourselves in the Lord . . . not vainly

looking on that prophecy in Daniel, 'And the Kingdom shall not be delivered unto another people.' "[34]

All the descriptions of the coming of the New Order in some way included the Jews, though few agreed on what their precise role was to be. Some relied on a text from the prophets in claiming that the Jews needed to be gathered together in Palestine as a prerequisite to the coming of the Messiah,[35] but most used another Old Testament text to uphold the proposition that he would arrive only when the Jews had been dispersed to every corner of the world.[36] The latter view easily accommodated the resettlement of Jews in England, since their absence necessarily forestalled the Messianic arrival.

The report of a Jewish traveler that the American Indians were found to be descendants of the ten lost tribes of Israel excited partisans of both theories among the Fifth-Monarchy Men, as well as numerous other Englishmen. Those who argued for total dispersal were able to maintain, convincingly if not logically, that the discovery of Jews in the New World was evidence in support of their theory. The opposition felt its claim strengthened, in that now no obstacle existed to the wholesale ingathering of all the twelve tribes. England and America were deluged with a "shower of pamphlets and tracts" relating to the report.[37] Increase Mather carried on a lively correspondence with Europe on the subject,[38] and even the conservative theologian Thomas Fuller was ready to lend some tentative credence to the notion.[39] In Holland, Menasseh Ben Israel accepted the thesis with alacrity, if not without some measure of skepticism, and wrote of it to his Fifth Monarchist friends, of whom he had many.[40]

Messianism, as was noted earlier, was a phenomenon widespread among Jews as well as Christians during this period. Desperation spread from Russia, where the Jews endured barbarous pogroms at the hands of the Cossacks under Chmelnitzki, to the Jews throughout Europe. It spread too, from Spain, where the Marrano Community of Jews who masqueraded as converts to Christianity was being unmasked by the Inquisition. Its pain was in part assuaged by the Messianic dream of terrestrial and temporal redemption. Protestants on the continent who were driven to Messianism by the ravages of the Thirty Years' War identified their cause with that of their Jewish counterparts. As Trevor-

Roper has observed, "In their hour of despair many of them decided to pool their Scriptures and amalgamate their Messiahs."[41] Jewish interest in the mystical and Kabbalistic book, *Sefer Ha'-Zohar* (the Book of Brightness), was revived as the Kabbalistic systems of numerology by using numerical values assigned to each Hebrew letter and then used the systems to predict the exact date of the Messiah's arrival. By almost general agreement, it was found by Hebrew scholars to be 1648. Various Fifth Monarchists, calculating by different means, put the date at 1655 or 1660[42] and others predicted the date of the Jews' conversion—the prelude to the Messiah's appearance—as 1650 or 1656.[43] Clearly, something was bound to happen during that decade.

More advanced philosemites demonstrated their feelings either by actually converting to Judaism or by at least proclaiming themselves Jews and observing the ceremonies. Several "Judaising sects" appeared in seventeenth-century England, the Traskites being one group about which most is known.[44] The founder, John Traske, was born in Somersetshire around 1583. He became a schoolmaster, and when imprisoned for his extreme Puritan views, undertook the study of Greek and Hebrew in jail. He eventually converted, moved to London in 1617, and acquired a following. In 1618, probably on Parliamentary urging, the Court of Star Chamber had him whipped, pilloried, branded with a J (for Jew), and fined £1,000. His sentence also included being served pig's meat while in jail. His wife, whom he had converted, and some of his followers were similarly incarcerated. Finding confinement not to his liking, however, Traske soon recanted his beliefs, subsequently becoming a stalwart Antinomian. His wife never was released, her last request being that she be buried in a field rather than in a Christian cemetery.

One of Traske's disciples, Hamlet Jackson,[45] experienced conversion even before he had encountered Traske. While on a journey one Saturday, he suddenly saw "the shining light of the Law around him" and ever after regarded the seventh day as one of rest. In 1618, along with one Christopher Sands, Jackson went to Amsterdam, where he was circumcised and received into the Jewish community of that city.

Traskite practices were as close to those of Hebrew ritual as might have been expected of men who knew little of the religion aside from the Old Testament, which they endeavored to interpret strictly. They followed the laws of the Jewish Sabbath, not kindling fires or cooking; they even abided by the dietary laws and ate no pig or meat uncleansed of blood. One observer—watching from a nearby jail cell—even reported a great squabble among the leaders over a point of Passover ritual which none seemed quite to comprehend.

The influence of the Traskites was apparently quite considerable, within London at least. Lord Chancellor Bacon made the telling comment:

> New opinions spread very dangerous, the late Traske a dangerous person. Prentices learn the Hebrew tongue . . . You will not think what a number of foolish followers he hath in this town and some other parts and yet he hath not been long of this opinion. He and divers of them are in prison, but continue obstinate, whereby a man may see there can arise no such absurd opinion but shall find followers and disciples.[46]

In 1621, Parliament expelled one of its members, Thomas Shepherd, on suspicion of being a Traskite. By the beginning of the next century, the sect had modified its beliefs slightly and came to be known merely as Seventh-Day men. Charles Whiting, writing in 1931, has observed that London's Old Mill Yard Church, which was descended from the Traskites, was still operating—holding services, to be sure, on Saturdays.[47]

Among the other sectaries, George Foster, a leading Fifth Monarchist, claimed that God during the course of a 22-hour trance had changed his name to Jacob Israel Foster. He prophesied that the Jews "would return to their own city and the Lord would reign in Mount Zion."[48] Winstanley and John Everard, entering an audience with General Fairfax (who was then investigating the Diggers' Cobham experiment), refused to remove their hats to Foster because "he was but their fellow creature" and they were also "of the race of the Jews."[49] Robert Rich, born of a wealthy family, became a disciple of the famous Quaker and self-styled Paraclete, James Nayler, in 1655. When Nayler was imprisoned for heresy, Rich, using the name of Mordecai, petitioned Parliament for his release "on behalf of the seed of the Jews," praying "that persecution might cease."[50]

Instances are numerous also of individuals whose philo-semitic leanings brought them privately to conversion. In 1624, for example, James Whitehall was imprisoned for preaching Judaism at Christ Church, Oxford.[51] The Puritan divine Nathaniael Holmes—who was incidentally one of Menasseh's correspondents —offered "to become the servant of Israel and serve him on bended knees," in keeping with prophetic text.[52] A Burgundian Jew who married a British woman, converted her and translated the important parts of the Jewish liturgy into English for her benefit.[53] Anne Curtyn was discharged from prison in 1649 after being held for having been "a professed Jew and causing children to be circumcised [sic]."[54]

Examples of more moderate philosemitism are evident among certain groups that adopted Jewish customs without going so far as to call themselves Jews or believers in Judaism. One contemporary chronicler by the name of Pagitt mentions the Sabbatarians and the Seventh-Day Baptists, for instance, who observed Saturday as well as Sunday as a day of rest.[55] This same reporter mentions a sect called Ethiopians that did the same.[56] Indeed, the sects in general tended toward a revival of the Jewish Sabbath.[57] Although they observed only Sunday as a holy day, the main body of Puritans applied to it some of the more restrictive features of the Jewish Sabbath, making it a day of prayer and abstention from work and amusement. It ought to be noted, however, that the Puritans neglected entirely the joyous aspects of the Jewish Sabbath, characteristically encouraging fasting on that day, for example, which Jewish law explicitly prohibits.

The Puritan custom of holding roundtable discussions[58] to debate sermons recently delivered in Church is similar to the Talmudic traditions of scholars holding like colloquies to interpret the laws of the Old Testament. The custom was never carried to the extreme point to which the Jews brought it, namely treating the body of interpretation itself as law and then erecting upon it a second body of interpretation. One book printed in the late sixteenth century, and authored in effect by a "committee" of divines who speak as if they are theological ancestors of the Independents, indicates that the similarity was not unnoticed. This treatise, entitled *The Brownists Synagogue,* describes the order of the Brownist service: two or three members arrive at a time, a "teacher" stands in the center of the room and prays on behalf of the whole congregation. Someone then delivers a sermon of about an hour's length, and then another "stand(s) up to make the text more plain."[59]

Amateur scholarship was supplemented by a rather intensive academic variety. Centered at Oxford primarily, and at Cambridge to a lesser degree, Hebraists began to appear at the universities in the middle of the sixteenth century. In 1597, Philip Ferdinand, who taught at both schools, published a book on Mosaic Law which received wide attention. Soon after, a professing Jew named Jacob Bartlett lectured with distinction at Oxford until he was forced to flee the country to avoid conversion. By the reign of James I, Hebraists of considerable ability and skill—their translation of the Bible bears witness—were disseminating in England knowledge of the Hebrew tongue and related subjects.[60]

As Puritanism increased in popular acceptance, Hebrew erudition grew apace. In 1637, the catalogue of a famous bookseller and collector contained one page of Hebrew titles. Ten years later Hebrew entries filled nine pages.[61] In the five years between 1648 and 1653, no less than nine Hebrew grammars were published.[62] Parliament recognized the interest in Hebraica sufficiently to vote £500 in 1647 to purchase for the Cambridge library a number of books in Hebrew and in other Eastern languages. Apart from Bibles, some 400 works were included.[63] By the middle of the century, according to the scholar de Sola Pool, "academic Hebrew learning . . . flourished indigenously in the sequestered cloisters of Oxford and Cambridge . . ."[64] This flowering was tended both by converted Jews[65] and by the "famous band of Christian scholars" headed by John Lightfoot and John Selden.[66]

Every university-trained cleric as well knew at least some Hebrew. The leading religious member of the Fifth Monarchists, John Rogers, wrote in 1653 *Ohel* (tent) *or Bethshemesh* (house of the sun), *a Tabernacle for the Sun,* in praise of the Independents over the Presbyterians. Even in America, Hebrew studies were being encouraged with some success, largely the result of efforts by Increase Mather.

The measure of the influence which the Hebraists exerted in

England may be crudely taken by comparison to their influence
in France and in America. Their influence in America was certainly considerable, but it was exceeded greatly by their counterparts in England.[67] The same is true of France. A catalogue of
French Hebraists issued in 1665 listed only 150, and Catholic
France never produced nearly the abundance of the quality of
scholars that Puritan England did. Only a few, like Bossuet,
were ever significant in France, whereas England abounded with
many scholars of the first water and many more of lesser note.

Graetz surely exaggerates when he writes that "the only thing
wanting to make one think himself in Judea was for the orators in
Parliament to speak Hebrew,"[68] but philosemitism was in fact
of considerable scope. Wherever the Puritan and sectarian
spirits reached, philosemitism made its inroads. As early as 1600,
the Bishop of Exeter voiced complaints of "Jewism" in his dio-
cese.[69] In the 1620's, Traskism excited much attention. Roger
Williams' *Bloody Tenent of Persecution*, which appeared in 1643,
was widely read and expressed strong sympathy for the Jews.[70]
In February, 1649, Edward Nicholas published his Apology for the
Honourable Nation of the Jews, which enjoyed "wide circulation
and influence." Nicholas called the expulsion a gross sin, absolved
the Jewish people of blame for the crucifixion, and urged kindli-
ness towards the persecuted.[71]

A few years later, Thomas Thorowgood clearly indicated the
extent of philosemitism in an illuminating prefatory note to
*Jews in America, or Probabilities that the Americans are of that
Race* (1652): "Lest any should conceive me also to Judaise, and
to be in love even with the wanderings of the unhappy people, I
will here profess I am not perfectly reconciled to them."[72] Why,
one might ask, does Thorowgood include this disclaimer clause?
Very simply, one might reliably conjecture, because Judaising was
sufficiently common to make Thorowgood wary lest he be taken
for one of its practitioners. As has been shown, philosemitism
appeared in many guises, and in many degrees; Thorowgood held
to a modern philosemitic position and merely exercised reasonable
caution that he not be forced to a more radical one. Indeed, one
must admire Thorowgood's prudence when we observe Zachary
Crofton blithely dubbing John Rogers "Rabbi" three years later.[73]

Menasseh arrived in London in September, 1655, already well known to many Englishmen, and, unfortunately for his cause, linked in most minds to the millenarians. In 1650, he had published in Latin a book entitled *The Hope of Israel,* which quickly ran through several editions and translations, reaching England in the vernacular in 1652. The discovery of the lost tribes of Israel, he argued, portended fulfillment of that requirement for the coming of the Messiah which Scripture had stated concerning the total dispersion of the Jews. In 1652, these had been popular notions, and the man who voiced them shared in that popularity. By 1655, however, the temper of things had changed.

In 1653, when many members of the Barebone's Parliament had been ready to lift its statutes directly out of the Old Testament, philosemitism was at its height. But the majority of the Parliament, taking "realistic" positions, pulled back; and, within a short time the public had reacted decisively against the politics of enthusiasm. With this reaction, the crest of philosemitism passed, and its familiar and opposite counterpart, *anti*semitism, once again gained currency in the minds of Englishmen. Rumors were spread that the Jews were conspiring to purchase St. Paul's Cathedral and fashion it into a synagogue. A "Russian Jewish apostate" who had severed with the Cavaliers wrote numerous tracts which reawakened hatred for the "Christ-killers."[74] The likelihood of converting Jews to Christianity, which many advocates of resettlement had supposed, seemed diminished. Pessimists even suggested that the stream of conversions would flow in the opposite direction.

At the time of Menasseh's visit to Whitehall in December, 1655, excitement reached its peak. Opponents and proponents vied for the ear of the public and the government in petitions, pamphlets, and polemics. William Prynne produced his virulently antisemitic *Short Demurrer to the Jews,* which included the telling comment: "the people (are) so dangerously and generally bent to Apostasy, and all sorts of Novelties and Errors in Religion: and would sooner turn Jews, than the Jews Christians." He was answered by Thomas Collier's *A Brief Answer to some of the Objections and Demurs made against the coming in and inhabiting of the Jews in this Commonwealth,* containing "a plea on their behalf, or some arguments to prove it not only lawful but the duty of those whom it concerns to give them the liberty and protection (they living peaceably) in this nation."

Upon his arrival, Menasseh issued his "A Declaration to the Commonwealth of England," in which he put forth the reasons for his mission, "in which millenary motives, the good of his own people, and the profit of the country as a whole were nicely balanced." According to Cecil Roth, his biographer, Menasseh refuted the premises for Gentiles' fear of Jewish proselytizing, economic unscrupulousness, and "ritual murder" of Christians, while demonstrating that his people's presence brought profit to the general community.[75] His formal petition, which was presented with Cromwell's approval to the Council of State on November 12, 1655, requested that the Jews be readmitted and allowed, on the whole, to order their own affairs with the supervision and protection of the state. Thinking the petition too controversial to be disposed of by themselves alone, the Council established a Conference of public and private interests to determine its fate. When the Conference assembled for its hearings on December 4th, it was composed of some of England's leading men, of whom sixteen were theologians, eight were merchants, eight were associated with government, and two were lawyers. Cromwell chaired the five sessions, which were held between December 4th and December 18th.[76]

This body was not so unfavorable to the petition as was the general populace. Cromwell, himself, concerned to diminish the capital resources of England's fierce trade competitors, the Dutch, was one of its most vigorous supporters. Men such as Oxford's John Owen and the Baptist Henry Jessey were representative of the liberal body of theologians, and Cromwell controlled the representatives of officialdom. The two lawyers dispassionately stated at the Conference's first session that no legal barriers existed to resettlement. It was the merchants who contributed strenuous opposition. The Jews would provide serious competition in trade, they argued, meanwhile, appending the list of scurrilities to which the public was accustomed to hear. The public, in fact, "keyed up to a considerable pitch of excitement by Prynne's *Demurrer,* which was now in every hand," packed the Whitehall Council Chamber at its last meeting, December

18th, when it was proposed that the Jews be readmitted, but
severe restrictions were passed which would have made Jewish
immigration unlikely in any case. According to Roth, neither
Menasseh's friends nor his enemies were willing to accept the
proposal, and Cromwell dismissed the committee without so much
as a motion to adjourn.[77]

Although a formal resolution to the problem was not reached,
Cromwell soon took action on his own initiative. In December,
1656, a house in Cree-Church Lane was converted into a synagogue, and soon thereafter the little congregation was able to
acquire a burial ground. A Hamburg Jew had already been admitted to take charge of the congregation. The London Exchange
soon admitted a Jew without requiring him to make the usual
affirmation of Christian faith. The reanimation of Jewish community life thus depended, after all, not upon law but rather
upon readiness of the general community to accept it.

We have already discussed both the nature and the extent of
the philosemitic sentiment which operated in favor of the Jews'
being readmitted to England; the strength of its opposition has
also been noted. When the bludgeoning of Prynne and the agile
sparring of Thorowgood and Crofton are considered, one may get
a fairly clear notion of the intensity of the battle and of the
closely balanced strengths of the adversaries. Despite many
favorable signs and conditions, however, the opposition won its
victory at the Whitehall Conference in December, 1655, but it
was a short-lived victory, and at best, existed in their own minds.
What must surprise us today is not the failure of Menasseh and
his supporters, but their near triumph.

Popular sentiment generally must be content to endorse or
to veto public policy; it is seldom that it can initiate it. Nor was this
an instance of that rare phenomenon. Had it not been for the
receptivity of a large body of popular opinion, the battle begun
by Menasseh could not have been won so soon.

NOTES TO CHAPTER II

1. Wolf, Lucien, "Crypto-Jews under the Commonwealth," in *Transactions of the Jewish Historical Society of England,* I (1893-1894), 56.

2. Graetz, H., *History of the Jews* (Philadelphia: Jewish Publication Society of America, 1895), V, 49.

3. The most important of modern Jewish messianic movements, known as Sabbatianism after its central figure, Sabbatai Zvi, had begun in 1648. It attained larger proportions throughout the 1650's and came to its climax in the following decade. In 1666, when presented by the Turkish Sultan with the alternatives of martyrdom or conversion to Islam, Sabbatai Zvi chose the latter. Although Jewish communities throughout the world were stunned and nearly shattered, and Sabbatai's name became a scandal, small groups of his loyal adherents maintained their faith in his Second Coming, a faith their descendants kept up for centuries.

4. Cf. the argument of Thomas Fuller, in his book *A Pisgah Sight of Palestine,* and of William Prynne's *Demurrer to the Jews,* both of which are discussed in the essay.

5. For extensive discussion of the economic issues involved, see Werner Sombart, *The Jews and Modern Capitalism,* tr. M. Epstein (London: T. Fisher Unwin, 1912).

6. From the "Westminster Confession" (1647). Quoted in Max Weber, *The Protestant Ethic and the Spirit of Capitalism,* tr. Talcott Parsons (New York: Scribner's, 1930), 100.

7. Cf. Weber, *op. cit.,* 117.

8. *Ibid.,* 162.

9. For the "rationality" of this process, see A.S.P. Woodhouse, *Puritanism and Liberty* (London: J.M. Dent and Sons, 1951), 94.

10. ". . . the Lord said to Isaiah . . . Go, and strip the cloth from your loins and remove your shoe from your foot . . . Isaiah walked naked and barefoot three years as a sign. . . ."

11. Whiting, Charles Edward, *Studies in English Puritanism from the Restoration to the Revolution, 1660-1688* (London: Macmillan Company, 1931), 192-3.

12. *Ibid.,* 243.

13. Graetz, *op. cit.,* 26.

14. Hyamson, Albert B., *A History of the Jews in England* (London: Methuen, 1938), 130.

15. Phillips, Henry, "An Early Stuart Judaising Sect," *Trans. of the Jew. Hist. Soc. of England* (1938), XV, 65. This name is taken from Hos. 5:14, where the Lion symbolizes the instrument of Divine retribution.

16. Hyamson, *op. cit.,* 130.

17. Graetz, *op cit.,* 26.

18. Sabine, George H., in introduction to the *Works of Gerard Winstanley* (Ithaca: Cornell University Press, 1941), 2.

19. "Truth Lifting up its Head" (1648), in *Works*, ed. Sabine, 128.

20. *Ibid.*, 521.

21. D. B. Robertson, *The Religious Foundations of Leveller Democracy* (New York: King's Crown Press, 1951), 119.

22. *The Out-Cryes of Oppressed Commons*, 14. Quoted in Robertson, *op. cit.*, 80. Although they claimed that anarchy existed in their rhetoric, "they continued to appeal to the laws of the land . . . they did not act as though society and government were dissolved." Robertson, 81.

23. Roberston, *op. cit.*, 59.

24. *Ibid.*, 61.

25. Brown, Louise Fargo, *The Political Activities of the Baptists and Fifth Monarchy Men in England During the Interregnum* (Baltimore: Lord Baltimore Press, 1912), 38.

26. Schenk, W., *The Concern for Social Justice in the Puritan Revolution* (London: Longmans, Green and Co., 1948), 136. This curious Parliament did indeed contain a number of "saints," or "godly party," such that "on one occasion a vote could not be taken because too many members were praying at the Blackfriars," the spiritual center of that group.

27. Jones, Rufus M., *Mysticism and Democracy in the English Commonwealth* (Cambridge, Mass.: Harvard University Press, 1932), 19.

28. Hyamson, Albert M., "The Lost Tribes and the Return of the Jews to England," *Trans. of the Jew. Hist. Soc. of Eng.*, V (1903), 143. Sadler was intent on finding a parallelism between the English Constitution and the laws of old Israel. The twelve-man jury he noted was of Jewish and Chaldean origin. Also, he observed the basis of the doctrine of excommunication in the Jewish *cherem*. He was the first to hint at the likelihood of the Britons' being descended from Israelitish ancestors, remarking that the ancient Druids practiced rites similar to those of the Canaanites, and that the word *Britain* was of Phoenician derivation.

29. See supra, 7.

30. Jordan, W. K., *The Development of Religious Toleration in England* (Cambridge, Mass.: Harvard University Press, 1938), IV, 34.

31. *Tracts on Liberty of Conscience and Persecution, 1614-1661*, ed. Edward Bean Underhill (London: Hanserd Knollys Society, 1846), I, 21.

32. Hyamson, *History of the Jews in England, op. cit.*, 137; cf. P. G. Rogers, *The Fifth Monarchy Men* (London: Oxford University Press, 1966).

33. Brown, *op. cit.*, 30.

34. *Ibid.*, 14.

35. Graetz, *op. cit.*, 23.

36. *Ibid.*, 28; see Daniel 12:7 and Deuteronomy 28:64.

37. de Sola Pool, David., "Hebrew Learning Among the Puritans of New England Prior to 1700," *Publications of the American Jewish Historical Society*, XX (1911), 81.

38. *Ibid.*, 60.

39. *A Pisgah Sight of Palestine* (1650) (London: William Tegg, 1869), 628.

40. Graetz, *op. cit.*, 23-4.

41. Trevor-Roper, H. R., "Philo-semitism," Horizon II, 4 (March, 1960), 102), see also Cecil Roth, *A History of the Marranos* (New York: Meridian Books and Jewish Pub. Soc. of America, 1959).

42. Brown, *op. cit.*, 23.

43. *Ibid.*, 15. Trevor-Roper's contention that philosemitism was imported to England by Messianist refugees from the continent seems to me indefensible in view of the facts that (1) there was strong evidence of the sentiment before the influx of refugees, and (2) its origins, as has been shown, were even more to be found in non-Messianic Puritanism.

44. Phillips, *op. cit.*, 63.

45. Roth seems to think that Hamlet Jackson was two men, since he writes "the Traskites Hamlet and Jackson. . . ."

46. Phillips, *op. cit.*, 67.

47. See Whiting, *op. cit.*, 314-6 and Phillips, *op. cit.* Both have drawn their accounts from the papers of the heresiographer Ephraim Pagitt.

48. Whiting, *op. cit.*, 234.

49. Winstanley, *Works,* George Sabine, ed. 15.

50. Fell-Smith, Charlotte, "Robert Rich" in *Dictionary of National Biography,* XVI, 1019.

51. Phillips, *op. cit.*, 63.

52. Graetz, *op. cit.*, 27.

53. Singer, S., "Early Translations and Translators of the Jewish Liturgy in England," *Trans. of the Jew. Hist. Soc. of Eng.* I (1893-4), 40. The original source is John Evelyn's Diary of 1641.

54. Phillips, *op. cit.*, 72.

55. Whiting, *op. cit.*, 319.

56. Pagitt, Ephraim, *Heresiography,* 3rd ed. (London: 1646). I might mention that there is now in Ethiopia a sect called Falashas, which has practiced Judaism for centuries in one form or another. What the connection between Pagitt's sect and the name of the African country might be one can only conjecture.

57. Whiting, *op. cit.*, 89.

58. *Ibid.*, 448.

59. Burrage, Champlin, *The Early English Dissenters* (Cambridge: Cambridge University Press, 1912), I, 207.

60. Roth, Cecil, *A History of the Jews in England* (Oxford: The Clarendon Press, 1941), 146-8, *passim.*

61. Abrahams, I., and Sayle, C. E., "The Purchase of Hebrew Books by the English Parliament in 1647," *Trans. of the Jew. Hist. Soc. of Eng.,* VIII (1914), 65.

62. Jordan, *op. cit.*, III, 209.

63. Abrahams and Sayle, *op. cit.*, 68-9. Interestingly enough, the funds

were taken from the monies set aside for the payment of the Scottish armies.

64. de Sola Pool, *op. cit.*, 35.

65. *Ibid.*

66. Abrahams and Sayle, *op. cit.*, 75.

67. de Sola Pool, *op. cit.*, 81-3. de Sola Pool contends that the strong Old Testament spirit in America was a Hebrew spirit. It is quite true that many scholarly figures were concerned with the Hebrew tongue—Governor Bradford, Increase Mather, *et al.*—but he does not adequately demonstrate that the popular spirit was similar.

68. Graetz, *op. cit.*, 27-8.

69. Roth, *op. cit.*, 149.

70. Wolf, Lucien, "American Elements in the Resettlement," *Trans. of the Jew. Hist. Soc. of England*, II (1899), 78-9.

71. Jordan, *op. cit.*, III, 211. The *Apology* appeared only two months after the first official move had been made toward restoring the position of the Jews. In December, 1648, the Council of Mechanics, meeting at White-hall, voted a resolution of religious toleration to extend to the Turks, Catholics, and Jews. The resolution was taken in response to a petition on behalf of the Jews submitted by Johana and Ebenezer Cartwright, non-Jews then living in Holland.

72. Quoted in Hyamson, "The Lost Ten Tribes," *loc. cit.*, 144.

73. See *supra*, 16.

74. Roth, Cecil, *A Life of Menasseh Ben Israel* (Philadelphia: Jewish Publication Society of America, 1934), 238-9.

75. *Ibid.*, 229.

76. *Ibid.*, 232-6.

77. *Ibid.*, 236-47.

III

Aesthetics of Modernity

1. *Augustinian Aesthetics Revisited*

I

When Augustine was a young man, he tells us in his *Confessions*, he asked himself and his friends

> "Do we love anything, but the beautiful? What then is the
> beautiful? and what is beauty? What is it that attracts and
> wins us to the things of love? for unless there were in them
> a grace and beauty, they could by no means draw us into
> them. And I marked and perceived that in bodies them-
> selves, there was a beauty, from their forming a sort of
> whole, and again, another from apt and mutual correspon-
> dence, as of a part of the body with its whole, or a shoe
> with a foot, and the like. And this consideration sprang
> up in my mind, out of my inmost heart, and I wrote *On the
> Fair and the Fit,* I think two or three books. Thou knowest,
> O Lord, for it is gone from me, for I have them not, but
> they are strayed from me, I know not how.[1]"

St. Augustine tells us that he did not regret the loss of this separate
treatise, yet the problems it examined remained among the most
persistent themes of his discourses, turning up in such works as his
epistles, sermons, diverse questions, commentaries on Scripture, and
throughout the whole range of his doctrinal writings and polemics.
In fact, it seems likely that his disregard grew out of a conviction
that a study of the beautiful, in a world so manifestly filled with
pleasing things, must overflow any arbitrarily imposed limitations,
and address itself to the larger examination of *all* beings, their

meaning, and the nature of men's response to them. Thus, as
Jacques Maritain observed in his study of the Schoolmen's theory
of art, "We must go to the Metaphysics . . . to discover what
their views were concerning the Beautiful, and then proceed to
meet Art and see what comes of the junction of these two terms."[2]

Ideally, this procedure—which I have made my own—has
the twofold merit of preserving the unity of the subject, and at
the same time, of illuminating some specific aspect of it. Certainly
it is the approach St. Augustine invites us to use in *De Doctrina
Christiana*. There, he introduces the subject of literary expression by very subtly distilling distinctions essential to this argument
in a brief discrimination between 'beings' and 'images' of beings.
Underscoring the metaphysical implications of these terms, he
says that all doctrine essentially concerns these two categories,
for that which is neither is nothing at all. Thus, to distinguish
between images, on the one hand, and nothing, on the other, is to
suggest that images also possess being insofar as they imitate it.
There are, then, two aspects from which to consider the image: one
can consider its meaning, from the point of view of the being it
signifies; or one can consider what might be called its "form," or
the being which it possesses in itself, insofar as it reflects it.[3] It
should, however, be emphasized that these categories are, in the
first place, artificial, and, in the second, relative: that is, they are
isolated from a single phenomenon which, when treated organi-
cally, must take *both* aspects into account.[4] With this *caveat* in
mind, one can proceed to a consideration of images, first as signs,
then as beings.

II

Although it is true to say, as has been noted, that every image
is also a being, it does not follow that every being is also an image,
an especially important exception since it describes God, who
is the ultimate and truly objective determinant, for imitation. That
is why, Augustine would doubtless assert, He never gave any
other image for Himself in Scripture. "The angel, and through the
angel the Lord Himself, said to Moses when he asked His name,
'I am Who Am.' "[5] He is, then, the fountainhead of being and
has made all other created things to imitate his fulness, in varying

degrees. Thus it is correct to say that all these are images of him, even though this term is usually reserved for man who, in his double nature as body and soul, most closely approximates God:

> Thanks to Thee, O Lord . . . We behold a face of waters gathered together in the fields . . . We behold the face of the earth decked out with earthly creatures, and man, created after Thy image and likeness, even through that Thy very image and likeness (that is the power of reason and understanding) set over all irrational creatures.[6]

In this sense, the whole created universe, as an image "means" the divine ideas that gave them form, in the remotely proportional way that words signify the thoughts of men, an analogy St. Augustine himself draws our attention to: "It is as when we speak. In order that what we are thinking may reach the mind of the listener through the fleshly ears, that which we have in mind is expressed in words and is called speech."[7] And as St. Augustine points out early in *De Doctrina Christiana*, words, from a very important point of view, are "signs whose whole use is in signifying. . . . For no one uses words except for the purpose of signifying something."[8] Furthermore, "no one should consider them for what they are, but rather for their value as images which signify something else. An image is a thing which causes us to think of something beyond the impression the image itself makes upon the senses."[9]

This radical dependence of "things" upon signs which signify transcendent meaning underlies an important aspect of St. Augustine's ideas about the proper nature of man's response to image and to being. Some beings, he says, are to be used, while others are to be enjoyed. To enjoy a being is to cling to it with love for its own sake. But the only proper object of love is Being itself, or God, so that by means of corporal and temporal beings we may comprehend spiritual and eternal ones.[10] St. Augustine illuminates this distinction through a metaphor of travel in which he refers to the image as a vehicle.

> Suppose we were wanderers who could not live in blessedness except at home, miserable in our wandering and desiring to end it and to return to our native country. We

would need vehicles for land and sea which could be used
to help us to reach our homeland, which is to be enjoyed.
But if the amenities of the journey and the motion of the
vehicles itself delighted us, and we were led to enjoy those
things which we should use, we should not wish to end our
journey quickly, and, entangled in a perverse sweetness,
we should be alienated from our country, whose
sweetness would make us blessed. Thus, in this mortal
life, wandering from native country where we can be
blessed we should use this world and not enjoy it.[11]

The most revealing illustration of these principles of the
nature and use of the image is found in one of St. Augustine's
own passages of Scriptural exegesis. The text he chooses to describe is from Canticles, and in it, the Church of Christ is imaged
as a beautiful woman: "Thy teeth are as flocks of sheep, that are
shorn, which come up from the washing, all with twins, and there
is none barren among them."[12] The spiritual meaning which is the
essential source of our enjoyment is explained by Augustine in the
following way:

> There are holy and perfect men with whose lives and
> customs as an exemplar the Church of Christ is able to des-
> troy all sorts of superstitions in those who come to it and
> to incorporate them into itself, men of good faith, true
> servants of God, who putting aside the burden of the world,
> come to the holy lover of baptism and, ascending thence,
> conceive through the Holy Spirit and produce the twofold
> love of God and their neighbour.[13]

If one can avoid the temptation to dismiss these passages as an
example of fantastic medieval exegesis, one can learn a good
deal from it. To begin with, the peculiar configuration of the
images themselves—teeth and sheep—do not lend themselves to
ready understanding or invite enjoyment on the level of sensible
recognition. They seem, rather, to demand some abstract pattern
of meaning which, as the earlier discussion would lead us to suspect,
lies wholly beyond the images it regulates. Besides illustrating
this radical dependence, however, the passage also underlines the

essential nature of the image-being relationship when it is discussed, as it has been here, solely in terms of meaning: the opposing terms of reference tend to resolve themselves into a simple dualism, a dualism which is accentuated by our sense of the incongruity that exists between them.

It is difficult, for example, to envisage holy men as the teeth of a beautiful woman; and even if such a response were possible, it is soon destroyed as we see her biting away the evil from men, chewing them to make them soft, and then digesting them. One is further shocked to find that the teeth become sheep which are shorn, dipped, and finally blessed with twins. To look at the passage in this way is to understand that the images in it function essentially as signs; and signs, as St. Augustine suggests elsewhere, bear an artificial or inorganic relationship to the meanings they signify.[14] That is, once meaning is achieved, there is no sense in which the sign itself is fulfilled: thus, teeth and sheep remain an order of experience our awareness of which is unchanged by the holy men whose acts are pointed to. Like the ship which St. Augustine referred to in a passage quoted above, the image as sign is used until we are brought to the country of meaning and then, presumably, dispensed with as a superfluous encumbrance.[15]

This dualism of meaning and vehicle is what the Middle Ages generally referred to as *allegoria*; the art of signifying one thing by saying something altogether and divergently different. But those who trace the rich tradition of mediaeval allegory to an Augustinian tradition, are, whatever the historical justifications, ignoring the warning St. Augustine himself pressed upon his readers; namely, that a discussion of images as signs of other things should not be confused with a discussion of images themselves.[16] Let us turn, then, to this other point of view and see how it complements what has been said thus far.

III

To begin with, we find that the rigorous distinction St. Augustine initially draws between the *enjoyment* of God's Being and the *use* of his created images in this world is not so absolute as it might at first seem, for he later goes on to say that "to enjoy" and "to use with joy" are very similar:

> When Paul wrote to Philemon, "Yea, brother," he said,
> "May I enjoy thee in the Lord."[17] If he had not added
> "in the Lord" but had said merely "I enjoy thee," he would
> have placed his hope of blessedness in Philemon. How-
> ever, enjoyment is very like use with delight. When that
> which is loved is near, it necessarily brings delight with it
> also.[18]

Thus while God is the object of man's enjoyment, the proper use
of those images which point to Him in time and space yields a
certain delight too. This delight may be thought of as an enjoyment arising from the temporal and corporeal similitude which
the image bears to the being it reflects, for what else can St.
Augustine mean when he speaks of that being as "near" when
represented in the image. This principle which underlines the
formal relationship of being and image is expanded in the comments surrounding the exegesis of the passage from Canticles.
There we are told that although the spiritual meaning St. Augustine paraphrases for us is very pleasant, yet for a reason he
does not understand, holy men are more pleasingly described for
him as the teeth of Christ's Church, even though this image says
nothing which is not said in the spiritual expression.

> But why it seems sweeter to me than if no such similitude
> were offered in the divine books, since the thing per-
> ceived is the same, is difficult to say and is a problem for an-
> other discussion. For the present, however, no one doubts
> that things are perceived more readily through similitudes
> and that what is sought with difficulty is discovered with
> more pleasure.[19]

In the last clause of his statement, St. Augustine seems to
suggest that the pleasure we take in discovering and apprehending the spiritual meaning is *enhanced* by the delight that is taken
in discovering the correspondence or relationship between the
meaning and its literal image: "what is sought with difficulty is
discovered with *more* pleasure." Although this matter is formidable, and refers, it seems, to a discussion outside St. Augustine's
immediate field of inquiry, it is possible to clarify some of its

implications by turning briefly to the metaphysical discussion of image and existence which introduces *De Doctrina Christiana*.

It will be recalled that God alone is there defined as true being, for He created all other things which may, therefore, truly be said to be images of Him. In this sense, the whole universe may be thought of as an order of images which signify His meaning, just as words signify the ideas of a speaker. This analogy is one which is deeply rooted in the Scriptural tradition of Hebraic-Christian philosophy, and St. Augustine draws deeply upon it to illustrate the distinctions and relationships between being and image. He uses, for instance, the opening passage from the Gospel of St. John, where God is imaged as a perfect Being who, in his relationship to the created universe, is a divine Poet, or the fountainhead of the Word in its double aspect as both meaning and form. The Word thus exists ideationally in God's ultimate Self and substantially in His literal creation, in what St. Augustine elsewhere refers to as God's universal song or poem ("carmen universitatis"),[20] with a particular shape, rhythm and harmony, just as the "Deus creator omnium" verse from St. Ambrose's hymn is shown to have formal proportions.[21] Like the individual words constituting the poem as a whole, the sky, the earth, and the humble creatures which inhabit it similarly have their own form; each, as it were, is modulated into long and short syllables. And like the separate images in Genesis, each of these discrete parts is good and delightful.

But if each distinct "word" is good, how much better is the entire poem which, in its completeness, not only reveals a fuller form and meaning, but also increases the delight we take in the separate words, revealing as it does their entire import through relations with the rest of the poem, and in this sense, fulfilling them. Thus, St. Augustine notes that

> ... of the several kinds of Thy works, when Thou hadst said "let them be," and they were. Thou sawest each that it was good. Seven times have I counted it to be written, that Thou sawest that which Thou madest was good: and this is the eighth that Thou sawest every thing that Thou hadst made, and behold, it was not only good, but also very good, as being now altogether.[22]

And elsewhere, this is added:

> That is not to be passed over lightly which is said, and
> "God saw all things which He had made, that they were very
> good." For when he was speaking of individuals, he said
> only, "God saw that it was good;" but when all were spoken
> of, it was too little to say "good" unless there were added
> "very." For if the several works of God, when they are
> considered by thoughtful persons, each with itself and its
> kind, to have excellent proportions and numbers and
> order, how much more altogether, i.e. the universe itself,
> which is composed of these several things collected into
> one. For, all beauty, which consists in parts, is much more
> commendable as a whole than in part; as in the human
> body, if we commend the eyes only or the several other
> beautiful points, singly and alone, how much more the
> whole body, to which all the members, being severally
> beautiful, contribute their beauty so that a beautiful hand,
> which being in the body was praised even by itself, if it be
> separated from the body, both itself loses its beauty, and
> the other parts, without it, are deformed.[23]

This matter, as St. Augustine tells us, is very important, for if
it does not actually demonstrate the formal being of the image, as
is the case, for instance, in *De Musica,* it does justify it by empha-
sizing the essentially organic relationship it bears to the order of
being. This organic relationship is underlined in the body-mind
analogy, a metaphor which tends to lead us away from the
artificiality of the sign, and towards another and essentially corporeal metaphor which is the model and informing principle of
all the being-image relationships in the created universe: I refer to
the archetypal Word, the incarnate Son, Who, being the perfect imitation of the Father, is the identical representation of the
one who begets Him, and was yet "made flesh and dwelt among
us."[24]

St. Augustine speaks of the nature of the mystery in the following passage:

> I acknowledge a perfect man to be in Christ; not the body
> of a man only, nor with the body and sensitive soul with-

out a rational, but very man; whom, not only as being a
form of Truth, but for a certain great excellency of human
nature, and a more perfect participation of wisdom, I
judged to be preferred before others. But Alypius imagined
the Catholics to believe God to be so clothed with flesh,
that besides God and flesh, there was no soul at all in
Christ, and did not think that a human mind was ascribed
to Him. But understanding afterwards that this was the
error of The Apollonarian heretics, he joyed in and was
conformed to the Catholic faith.[25]

In this figure, the superlatively good and the separate good, the
object of enjoyment and the image of delight are conjoined within
the terms of a single being: God and man, Who are the same in
Christ, even though the one is more excellent than the other. Within this conception, the radical dualism, like the Apollonarian
heresy, disappears. In fact, that is what we should have expected
from the beginning, for even when St. Augustine speaks of
images only in terms of what they mean, or refer to, he likens
them commonly to a "vessel," and in particular to a ship. In
selecting this figure, he is doubtless aware that St. Ambrose had
earlier compared that vehicle to the body of Christ, and also to
His Church which, at the conclusion of time, would rise to meet
its master, and be united with Him. Far from being abandoned at
the approach of ultimate meaning, the vessel becomes part of a fulfilled order which for Augustine, is "altogether both good and very
good."[26] Hence Christ speaks of his incarnation as a discrete
stage within a *unitary* and hierarchical experience:

The Lord created me from the beginning of his ways,[27]
so that those who wished to come might have *a beginning
in Him*. . . . Thus He says, "*I am the way,* and the truth,
and the life" that is, you are to come through me, to arrive
at me, and to remain in me. When we arrive at Him, we
arrive also at the Father[28]—since by an equal, another
equal is known.[29]

Thus, the images God has created in this world (together
with the images of human "creation," insofar as those acts imitate

its divine counterpart) are to be understood, like their archetypal model, "not allegorically, but properly," that is, figuratively.[30] To illustrate what he means, St. Augustine explores the meaning of the phrase, "increase and multiply" from the account of creation in Genesis. Though spoken of one creature, it is inferred in many, and the many are carefully catalogued within a specific hierarchical pattern, ascending from creatures of the sea, to creatures of land, from beasts to men, and from the corporeal to the spiritual (for "we find 'multitude' to belong to creatures . . . in heaven and earth").[31] In this sense, the divine principle is signified in the images of the created world, but these also participate in what is pointed to; the divine world not only manifests what is signified, but also perfects, in the sense of fulfilling what the image itself contains.

The polarity of simple signification is thus dissolved, and the incongruities between image and being, while not supplanted, are superseded by another awareness, one which makes for a striking "double knowledge" which is superbly manifested in this ironic comment from the fourth book of *De Doctrina Christiana,* where Augustine speaks of the relation of humble language to important ideas:

> Certainly, if we were advising men how they should act in worldly cases, either for themselves or for their friends, before ecclesiastical judges, we should rightly urge them to speak in a subdued manner as if of small things. But when we are speaking of the eloquence of those men whom we wish to be teachers of things which will liberate us from eternal evil or lead us to eternal good, wherever these things are discussed . . . they are great things. Unless, perhaps, because a cup of cold water is a small and most insignificant thing, we should also regard as small and most insignificant the promise of the Lord that he who gives such a cup to one of His disciples "shall not lose his reward."[32]

Although St. Augustine implies that images possess the broadest possible potential with regard to linguistics, to meaning, and to ultimate truth, and although this indeed must include a relationship to being which tends towards allegory, the essential relationship he describes possesses a rather different order of implications, implications which one might call, with St. Augustine, "figural" rather than allegorical, and should be characterized, if one may attach any importance to the passage above, by ironic complexity rather than by simple dualisms.

2. Milton's Hell and the Typology of Anonymity

What is a type, and how does Milton project his idea of type by means of his poetry? How does the idea become perceptible? And finally, what new empirical knowledge of the morphology of type can one derive from its image in Milton's poetry, and what light can this knowledge throw on the hidden mental and spiritual processes of life and the emergence and status of religious feeling, Christian experience, and concepts of the after-life in seventeenth-century England? The questions posed are far-reaching, and bring together a disparate assortment of information in designs perhaps unusual for Milton criticism; but it is suggested that the amount of significant thinking represented by Milton's poetry becomes more impressive as one ramification of the philosophical issue—Milton's construction of a typological concept of mind adequate to the phenomena of poetic experience—becomes explicit.

To start, then, with the most elementary questions: what does it mean to speak of a type? What is a projection of type, and what means does Milton employ to represent projections of type in his poetry? In general terms, the type is a concept which is part of a larger rational structure. Types are symbols of a conceptual order in which all possible elements constituting that order may be arranged or isolated so that any particular type may be unequivocally designated and any combination of sets of types may be distinguished and compared; it is largely by virtue of its particular location in a complex logical (relational) system that the type can present us with images of more complex subjective activity that it itself represents as an idiosyncratic symbol. Still in general terms, the type is a metaphorical representation of something negotiable: i.e., it may denote a projection of sensible or insensible conditions

of the world, states of mind, events, persons, or analogous phenomena, or when it is used as an exemplification (to distinguish
it from an instrument which exemplifies), the type may very
frequently make another, more obscure element in the large
relational system conceivable. In this context, it should be emphasized that all conceivable types in the same order exemplify a
basic principle of isomorphism—that is to say, the degree of
analogy or sameness in logical form between the type as conceived and the more elusive phenomenon which it represents is
obvious and usually perceivable. The type and its obscure
analogates also obey a principle of negotiability not entirely unlike
the principle which determines the negotiability of phenomena
which the type may denote: what may be conceivable as a symbolic exemplification at one point, may at another itself serve as
its own elusive symbol.

Now, to speak of a "projection" in terms of all of the circumstances which invest either the concept of "projection" or its
instrumental applications with metaphorical value does not
hardly exhaust its figurative uses; nevertheless, whether the disparate applications of the word refer to extension, circumstance,
instrumentation, action, or sensible psychology, each relates back
to a single principle of presentation: the enhanced perceptibility
of an object (or idea) or a feature of an object. In ordinary
life, this principle may operate with the "projector's" intention as
the instrumental force, or it may be unintentional, accidental,
spontaneous. With regard to a work of art, the act of making the
presentation (or the setting forth of the symbol) is usually considered to be intentional. It is for this reason that critics most often
characterize the work of art (or the symbol) itself as a projection
of what it symbolizes; thus, for the purposes of this essay, it will
be assumed that *Paradise Lost* is a projection of Milton's ideas into
some perceptible form. The general semantic theory of projection
and symbolic presentation is also taken for granted, for here I am
concerned with one of its special and extremely complex applications—the analysis of Milton's presentation of typological ideas.

But before moving directly to that, it would be of some use to
sketch in brief one of the simplest models of typological projection
in ordinary life so as to provide a kind of backdrop and analytic
touchstone for subsequent reference. With a thermometer, one

may project the change of temperature in observable terms by coupling the fluctuations in actual temperature with visible and perceivable changes in the level of mercury. This is made possible because of the factor of physical covariance, which not only gives the meter its instrumental character as a device that measures and determines actual temperature, but which functions, at the same time, as a symbol of a special, well-ordered conceptual system. Constituting a one-dimensional spatial continuum, all possible temperatures are symbolically projected as a single straight line, where the continuum of conceivable temperatures appears as visual exemplifications: a series of degrees of heat etched on a glass tube. When employed in mathematical languages, this kind of logical symbolism and symbolic projection is the extreme of literal expression; but in epistemology and art, it has hardly been touched, doubtless because of the great gulf that has been thought by many semanticists and logical positivists to exist between propositional and metaphysical language.

A type similarly represents the general in particular, and is an ontological concept. In ordinary life, typologizing is a basic characteristic of being in the world, because man visualizes himself and the natural world in a schematic way. He perceives phenomena as embodying a structural order, with differences in shading and outline, and so on. Thus, types arise from man's ability to perceive typical shapes. But typological perception is itself a phenomenon *sui generis*; it itself is an ideal existential norm, for if and when man succeeds in positioning himself in the world of the type's meaning by means of the intentionality of words and the intersubjectivity of gestures, man may transcend his natural power in such a way that the type's universality appears as typicality—only then true conformation to type becomes possible.

Man's experience institutes this transcendence within his world as a permanent possibility in much the same way as a work of art uses words to polarize man's existence (via subject and object) in a certain direction expressive of its intention. In effect, words which also happen to be types support their non-being; in general, *Paradise Lost* may be considered to be a poem which uses words in such a way: its types express and manifest an objectified subject-object unity in potential. Since type signifies the ideal form of a phenomenon, it is the essence of the subject-object unity; that is to say, the subject-object dichotomy no longer applies because the type itself arises from a contact between the totality of being and concrete phenomena—a contact, it should be emphasized, which may be realized over and over again when, say, one reads and rereads *Paradise Lost*.

Here it should be pointed out that the pure (or fulfilled) type-anti-type configuration in literature ideally results in the reader's mere, but immediate, awareness of the existence of the anti-type; in such an act of thought, the reader first posits the ideal existence (or former existence) of the figural attribute at a more or less specific point in the spatio-temporal continuum, though this ideal type is utterly anonymous relative to any existing person or any contemporary event or word. Similarly, Miltonic figures—for example those of Hell or of Satan—which cannot be apprehended except as ideal types, are also anonymous in this sense. This is so because each ideal type confronts time with an ambiguous actualization of its linguistic *qua* typical potential which is witnessed and inferred from all the predicates and attributives Milton uses to restrict the meaning of the type.

Hell's existence is, of course, not directly experienced by the reader, whether or not it be assumed, believed likely, or even taken for granted. Even with regard to the lord of the kingdom, and the reader's immediate experience of him in the poem, Satan may be understood to occupy the status of an individuated intersection of typical attributes. The reader may have explicit experiences of Satan's personality in any one of its multiple aspects. Of necessity, these experiences are nothing more or less than acts of thought on the reader's part by which Satan's existence as "Seabeast/Leviathan," (I.200-1) or "stripling Cherub," (III.636) or "Tiger," (IV.403) or "Toad, close at the ear of *Eve*" (IV.800) is imagined or apprehended (directly or indirectly) with respect to Satan's figural attributes. Given this fundamental identity between our experience of each of Satan's constitutive elements (represented conventionally in terms of image or emblem) and corresponding acts of thought, the reader's experience of Satan may be differentiated in various ways. One important way relates to the reader's sense that while his perceptions are almost always indirect, they are not equally anonymous. Indeed, one may observe as a general rule the phenomenon that the total body of the reader's experience of the figural world which constitutes *Paradise Lost* is stratified by the relative degree of concreteness or anonymity that characterizes the ideal type by which each type is apprehended. The more anonymous the ideal type that mediates the existence of a figure with recognizably human attributes, the more advanced is the substitution of objective matrices of meaning for the subjective meaning ascribed to the ideal type. Indeed, the more advanced the substitution, the more dependent, in turn, is the subjective ideal type constituting a given experience upon a substratum of (more or less) anonymous subjective ideal types and corresponding matrices of meaning.

The anonymity of an ideal type is a concept that requires further clarification. The function of Milton's typology in *Paradise Lost* is to establish, or more properly, to re-establish and validate a scriptural system of knowledge and salvation wherein history's symbolic relations may be related to their fulfillment in Christ— "disciplin'd/ From shadowy Types to Truth, from Flesh to Spirit" (XI.302-3). Once it is recognized that therein lies the manner in which "God with man unites" (XII.382), it becomes possible to speak of the type as a signification of the ideal aspect of all phenomena, historical as well as symbolic. In Scripture, in most seventeenth-century Puritan exegetics and covenant theology, as well as in *Paradise Lost* itself, this typologizing method proceeds deductively and by empirical means, relating multiplicity to the normative in such a way as to insure the location of an absolute existential norm in human history, a norm—it should be added—which is spoken out of human experience; and its goal, an application of typology's existential dialectic to man's own subjectivity in order to bring about a self-conformation to Christ in an anthropological move from one existence to another, a move, which, if completed, involves a self-transformation whose end is total incorporation and fulfillment in Christ. Kohelet expresses the process perhaps best by likening the type to the yeast in the dough, and to a principle of irritability without which the soul cannot rise. In this context, it should be noted that the character of the reader's subjective acceptance of Satan's existence is directly proportional to the character of the reader's active response to him, in comparison with experiences of, and actions toward, other humans in face-to-face orientation.

The concept, anonymity of the ideal type, may then be understood to refer to the relative scope of the typifying system; and the scope of the typifying scheme in *Paradise Lost* is determined by the relative completeness and generality of that portion of the stock of knowledge which guided Milton's selection of the particular quality to be typified as an invariant attribute within the typifying scheme. When, for example, the scheme is derived from what may be presumed to be Milton's previous experiences of a specific individual, event, or literary convention, the typification is relatively concrete. Examples of this form of figural scheme may be seen in Milton's description of Satan as a Leviathan who is mistaken by "The Pilot of some small night-founder'd skiff" for "some Island, oft, as Seaman tell,/ With fixed Anchor in his scaly rind," (I.204-6) and in Milton's comparison of the demons entering Pandemonium with bees—the emblem of the Barberini Pope Urban VIII—who, "In springtime, when the Sun with *Taurus* rides,/ Pour forth their populous youth about the Hive/ In clusters" (I. 768-771). When the typifying scheme is derived subjectively from ideal types available in Milton's stock of general doctrinal and theological knowledge concerning the ultimate realities of the natural world or of the transcendent world, it is relatively anonymous. This is the case, for example, when Milton has Eve utter the ultimately paradoxical though consolatory remark: "though all by mee is lost,/ Such favor I unworthy am vouchsaf't,/ By mee the promis'd Seed shall all restore" (XII.621-3); in effect, she is expressing her awareness once again that knowledge of death is a cognitive limit, and that she and her seed (collectively and as a group) constitute the initial, organic types of a redemptive arc which will be brought to completion by Christ, the ideal type of redemption.

These remarks should make six things obvious: 1) that the degree of concreteness of the typifying scheme in *Paradise Lost* is inversely proportional to the level of generality of those experiences sedimented in the stock of knowledge from which the scheme is derived; 2) that each cluster of type-anti-type involves other clusters of other typifications; 3) that the deeper the substrata of typifying schemes which are involved in a given ideal type, the more anonymous it is, and the larger is the region of things simply taken for granted in the application of the ideal type;

4) that the reader's knowledge of the individuals and events of the figure world of *Paradise Lost* is typical knowledge of typical processes; 5) that detached as they are from subjective configuration of meaning, such processes—typical experiences of "some" individual or "some" event—exhibit the idealization: "again and again," i.e., of typical anonymous repeatability; and 6) that the more likely it is to apprehend directly the ideal-typical characteristics of a figure such as Satan in *Paradise Lost* as elements of the ongoing conscious life of a concrete individual, the less anonymous are these traits. This final point concerning what may be termed the recognizability-conformability quotient of Milton's figures may be illustrated by two examples: the first, related to Satan; the second, to Hell itself.

In his Argument prefixed to Book II, Milton asserts the following concerning the "great consult" in Pandemonium: *"Satan* debates whether another Battle be to be hazarded for the recovery of Heaven: some advise it, others dissuade: a third proposal is preferr'd, mention'd before by *Satan*, to search the truth of that Prophecy or Tradition in Heaven concerning another world, and another kind of creature equal or not much inferior to themselves, about this time to be created: Thir doubt who shall be sent on this difficult search: *Satan* thir chief undertakes alone the voyage, is honor'd and applauded."

When a reader reflects upon Satan in this context, one is aware that Satan is facing a difficult decision. From former experiences of Satan's action and personality in Book I, one retains a memory of Satan as an ideal type in a general way; now, one may also form an action-pattern typification, "Satan's general attitude and conduct in the face of difficult decisions." This ideal type, too, is other-oriented in the sense that Satan is not a sort of creature who could exist in an I-Thou-orientation: " 'Others' like Satan are likely to behave in such a manner when they face difficult decisions." Still, the ideal type "my first experience of Satan" in any one of a number of his attributively human traits is highly concrete, based on direct experience in the past of humans "like" Satan in face-to-face situations. Furthermore, technical difficulties notwithstanding, one is also aware of the likelihood that humans manifesting attributively Satanic traits may be among one's contemporaries.

These observations are quite simple and not totally unexpected; with regard to the morphology of Hell as an anonymous
type, however, the issue of recognizability is far more complex.
Although there is some justice in assuming that Milton's idea of
Hell, indeed his special emphasis upon Satan, is meant to imply
the failure of God and the triumph over God by the powers of
darkness, it is nonetheless possible (although unjustified) to
recognize a transference to the divine life of the idea of the abuse
of freedom which is implied in man's moral and spiritual life. But
in this recognition and correspondence, there is a rationalization
of what is absolutely irrational. Furthermore, to call in aid the
idea of free will in defence of Milton's Hell a recognizable type
or type-anti-type cluster is to push the matter into the background;
it solves nothing, because neither the general idea of free will nor
the particular one of Pauline liberty is applicable to the concept
with which we are dealing.

Here, a distinction must be drawn between the psychology and
the ontology of anonymous types. As an anonymous type, a psychology of Hell is certainly admissible and even necessary. But
the concept of a prison, owned, prepared and constructed by God
for anonymous and numberless souls, is an idea of ontological
significance which, for Milton, is impossible and inadmissible.
In other words, to say that what man thinks of as that which is
possibly coming to God, Milton would consider already eternally
realized; i.e. the torments of Hell are already actual, since they
were part of the divine plan of creation. Hence to keep the subject
of Hell within the limited context of human reason (as every
ontology has been) is not Milton's intention. For if it were, Hell
could be understood only as an objectified and rationalized form
of human cruelty and suffering. It is in opposition to this that
Milton is asserting that the anonymity, and in this case, the non-
existence, of Hell is a moral postulate.

For Milton, uncertainty about the recognizability of Hell is
tied to the limitations of man's verifiable knowledge and to the
complexity of reality—to the uncertainty of the meaning of the
problematical in man himself. As an "historian" of man's history,
Milton is aware that the meaning of the history of Hell as either
an activity, state of mind, or ontological concept is bound to the
essential nature of that condition, and that the meaning of fulfilled

history is the meaning which man attaches to human existence and to the succession of forms that it takes through time. As for typological or figural schemes which set forth the succession of "historical" units, whether of Hell or of Paradise, they cannot be worth more than the units they bind together. In short, a proclamation of inevitable damnation cannot signify more than a definition of Hell. And these are the basic, one might almost say Gregorian, reasons why Milton constitutes his Hell in *Paradise Lost* with three ubiquitous physical hells and one non-localized "moral" Hell: the burning lake—"A Dungeon horrible, on all sides round/ As one great furnace flam'd, yet from those flames/No light, but rather darkness visible. . . ." (I. 61-3)—the Doric Palace of Pandemonium—"Built like a temple, where *Pilasters* round/Were set, and Doric pillars overlaid/ With Golden Architraves;" (I.713-15)—and the huge, frozen continent—"dark and wild, beat with perpetual storms/ Of Whirlwinds and dire Hail, which on firm land/ Thaws not, but gathers head, and ruin seems/ Of ancient pile; all else deep snow and ice,/ A gulf profound . . ." (II. 588-92).

In Genesis, the hierarchic universe of heaven and Hell is conceived largely in terms of temporal dimensions; each is a member of a "realized" eschatology. With this *bête noire* of Puritan theology in *Paradise Lost,* we are faced with what may be termed a "simultaneous" eschatology, particularly as far as the essential Hell is concerned; each physical sub-Hell has a certain objectified location which emphasizes the spatial rather than temporal, dimension of its local reality; but the fourth Hell, mentioned earlier, is of the psychical kind: Satan's mind is one "not to be chang'd by Place or Time." His "mind is its own place, and in itself/ Can make a Heav'n of Hell, a Hell of Heav'n" (I.253-5).

It is suggested that the existence of a non-localized moral and ethical Hell which exhibits a strict covariance and synonymy with the contents of Satan's mind represents Milton's efforts to cope with the difficult theme of moral and psychological evil; it is obvious, on the one hand, that Milton, like Calvin before him, conceived of the idea of Hell as being inseparably linked to the paradox of evil; but it is equally obvious, on the other, that when Milton has Satan declare "Which way I fly is Hell; myself am Hell;" (IV.75), Satan is expressing a scandalous message, for the evil he typifies is a scandal not only to man but to God. For almost inevitably, from Satan's perspective in the Renaissance hexameral tradition in which this *locus communis* is placed, God is held to be responsible for it. Milton's Satan becomes a weapon in the hand of God, and through him the ends of Providence are realized. No independent power is ascribed to Satan; he can do virtually nothing creative. Furthermore, the evil which his psychic condition embodies and projects is wholly negative; it has an illusory power simply because it steals from good.

Yet what is more significant in Milton's version of the Genesis myth is that evil is a consequence of the freedom which God imparted to Adam and Eve. There appears to be no rational way out of the contradiction which this paradox involves, for Milton's unrationalized way of understanding evil is above all else an attempt to interpret it as the testing of freedom. This notion is still in no way connected with any thought of an ontology expressed in concepts; rather, it is a description of spiritual experience. And this is perhaps a partial explanation of what is meant by the narrator's aim of justifying the ways of God to man, i.e. such a representation of evil is, in one sense, a justification of evil.

For Milton, then, freedom assumes the experience of evil—a moral paradox from which there appears to be no way out. It is only when the experience of evil is considered in the context of anonymous types, that a path out of this dilemma becomes visible. It becomes possible, for example, to conceive of an ethic of anti-Hell which "desires" the salvation of all men; that is to say, an ethic which holds out the ideal possibility of salvation for all of mankind—a concept which implies that even at the height of his progress, man may experience a fresh submergence in matter, but a submergence that cannot be ultimate in human destiny. This, then, is the resultant meaning of Milton's presentation of Hell as an anonymous type: because Hell exists only in time, and demonstrates the impossibility of issuing out of time, it cannot be transferred to eternity.

Accordingly, the theme of *Paradise Lost* as a whole illustrates the idea that the life of man which results from the original transgression in Eden ought to be understood not as if it were a legal process subject to forensic interpretation, but as a tragedy which is characterized by fate and freedom at the same time. Yet because *Paradise Lost* concludes on a note of optimism, with Adam accepting the legal sentence imposed upon him by God, it may be argued that there is virtually no tragic element in the idea of an eternal Hell, for Adam accepts and understands it as a sentence passed not so much from without but from within. So much for determinism but what is one to make of the apparently antinomian assertion that Adam's will is free to choose in very much the same way as his reason is? A reconciliation of Adam's freedom and fate is possible only if his freedom of will is asserted in order that the final sentence should *appear* just. It is only in this tragic way of understanding the judgment that evil may be entirely overcome, for it is an understanding which involves a freedom which gives rise to tragic conflict. This is perhaps a repulsive fact about *Paradise Lost,* but one which largely explains the reason why Milton seems to accept Hell entirely without any sense of tragedy, and even with a little satisfaction.

Rising above exoteric demonology represented in so many early hexameral poems, which maintain the notion that the eternal pain of Hell is the final expression of man's legalistic and utilitarian state of mind, Milton's Reformation epic manifests a spiritual recovery from the utilitarian idea of Hell. Indeed, it marks in poetic form the substitution of the ideal of Hell as a retributive instrument with the conception of the influence of clarifying spirit, of transfiguration, of the attainment of the knowledge of God's completeness—all of which involve the path of mortification and tragic conflict.

3. *Natural Facts and Poetic Insight*

Consider, as a tentative basis for discussion, the suggestion that the essence of all science can be regarded as the arranging of common experience into an order or pattern which is provisional and never final. Since poetry may also present a pattern from experience, the definition is worth pursuing. The scientific pattern may be a network of ideas mathematically expressed, as in the physical sciences, or it may be a set of descriptive logical classifications, as in the biological, mental and social sciences. All sciences like to call their patterns sequences of cause and effect, but the precise meaning of that term can be queried. In every case the "advance" of science, which is the superseding of pattern by pattern, occurs by bringing an ever wider range of facts under ever simpler categories. The proviso, that the experience be "common" experience, means that features individual or personal, or determined by local or transient circumstances are to be eliminated, and the pattern is to emerge as expressing only what is repeatable by successive observers and can be communicated by each observer to the other.

This eliminating of the personal creates the picture of an external "Nature" independent of its separate observers: this picture may or may not be ultimately an illusion. Thus the most general correlations of facts, laid bare as uniformities expressible in mathematical equations, are usually called Laws of Nature. "Nature" then becomes the abstraction from every man's experience, the sum total of all facts observed; so the word "supernatural" drops out of the scientific dictionary as self-contradictory. It could only denote an observing of what is not observable. To retain the word to denote what we do not yet *understand* is an artificiality which pleases some people; but we have little enough understanding of any ultimate substratum which may underlie observable Nature, and no modern scientist pretends to know what Nature is, apart from this restricted meaning of observed fact.

It is clear that this self-discipline of science must be radically separated from the self-discipline of the arts, because it makes personal emotional preference irrelevant. We do not accept or reject a numerical estimate of the electrical charge of an atomic particle because it would be pleasing or unpleasing to "believe," or because a mystic revelation has uncovered it to some authority, but because repeated impersonal experimenting enforces the high probability of its accuracy until better experimenting may amend it. So the probability of truthfulness grows with the variety of the experiments or observations which yield concordant figures; any law of Nature exemplified in a set of equations attains its slow arduous progress towards a provisional degree of "scientific truth" the wider the range of verifiable facts that can be expressed in those equations. That is why the sign of advance in science is the dissolviing of complex categories into ever simpler and fewer distinct notions, such as, for example, the interaction of electric fields.

An instance of some of these features is the mathematical physics of wave-motion, the kind of phenomenon of which obvious cases occur when water is disturbed or a stretched string is plucked; the law of vibrations and waves gains its generality when we find that light, X-rays, radio, and heat radiation can be shown to obey the wave-equation, as these phenomena exemplify the vibration of electrical and magnetic quantities. The more recent discovery that the behavior of electrons can also be formulated in the wave-equation is a further gain in unifying our pattern of the external world, since facts so widely scattered as to appear in medical chemistry, in astronomy, in electrical engineering, and in the study of the earth's interior or the earth's upper atmosphere, are all instances of the behavior of electrons.

But this describing of the electrons themselves by wave-equations introduces also a feature which gives to recent physics considerable novelty in its approach to the meaning of "knowledge." If concepts which previously were exclusive to the world of matter, such as the concept of the electron, have become examples of the wave-equation which had also described the world of radiation in empty space, the notion of "material" has lost the meanings given to it by the science of half a century ago, and has come to share the most characteristic property of the immaterial. So our regard for "substance" has been replaced by a regard for "symbol," and we utilize a symbolic wave-equation for calculating an experimentally verifiable fact without hoping or even desiring to picture a "thing" vibrating in the wave. We seek a pattern, and we no longer ask what it is pattern of or what it is pattern in. We are content to manipulate a mathematical structure if it yields observable fact, but remain happily agnostic about the ultimate nature of whatever exhibits that form or structure. One could be just as good a physicist without "believing in" the existence of a material world at all, certainly without supposing that nothing but a material world exists—a fancy dear to our scientific ancestors.

But if the "real" in any philosophy of physical science is no longer identifiable with the "material," I suggest that it may more nearly denote the "temporal." Radiation and matter are no longer

explained as if they were small-scale or fine-grain models or copies
of the large-scale objects of our perception. But because a space-
time frame or pattern is still our mode of expressing the resulting
experiences, we cannot evade the fact that if *matter* has lost
its primitive significance, *time* has not. Science is not interested
in a static universe but in the changes which give rise to observation; periodic changes such as reproduction of life or circulation
of planets or crystal growth, or catastrophic changes such as the
disruption of an atom or of a great star, or gradual and statistical
changes such as those we call evolutionary. In all these, the one
quantity inescapable which cannot be transformed away is the
"passage of time;" so the fundamental equations of physical
science, from the epoch of Newton or of Maxwell, or of today's
wave-mechanics of the atom, are all equations denoting variation
of some property with time. This is because the scientific account
is always a pattern based on the observer's experience, and the
most inescapable feature of Nature is that we experience only
events in a serial order—a more rational way of stating what
common language had called the "passage of time."

This unavoidable intrusion of Time emphasizes that science
as the arranging of some pattern from experience is always based
upon "sense-data." For its raw material is always supplied by
sight, hearing, touch, etc., and by these senses we detect only
alterations in our surroundings, not permanencies. This is still as
true today, when unaided senses are reinforced by telescope,
microscope, photographic or spectrographic plate, loudspeaker,
electrical meters and chronographs and oscillographs.

But the stage from impact of the world upon a human sense,
or upon a human-made instrument, to recognition of what the
sensation of sight or sound implies, introduces the unsolved
problem of perception. Perception, as involving the recognition
of what we suppose can cause those sensations, is impossible
except for an intelligence based on memory, and also on imagination or the power of creating a coherent mental vision. Take a
crude instance of this; while a coin is being looked at from different
angles our sight is presented with a succession of differing elliptic
shapes. Without memory and some power of imagination, the
several shapes would never synthesize into our recognition that
there is only one external object, the single circular coin whose

appearance from different angles is giving rise to the successive sensations of ellipses.

The physicist's translation of a sensation—for example, the sight of a mark on a photographic plate—into a decision that the path of an electron in a magnetic field denotes a given amount of energy, involves in principle no more mysterious a chain of mental processes than that which underlies the apparent miracle of recognizing the coin, or of recognizing a neighbor's face. The scientist's calculation of an atomic property, and his friend's daily recognition of a commonplace salutation, are both examples, in very differing complexity, of the way the mind builds concepts out of sense-data, imagery, and memory. They differ mainly in that the scientific concepts, such as "electromagnetic field," "electric charge," etc., are simple and of verifiable meaning, and therefore have to be free from the impress of the observer's complex individuality which would color everything by feeling and personality.

This very brief analysis of the relations between Sensation, Perception and Concept, may serve to illustrate our first statement that scientific knowledge is the making of pattern out of common or impersonal experience. This result must dominate the comparison of poetic with scientific attitude. The same analysis has also reinforced our statement that sense-data, underlying scientific as well as everyday experience, are the impermanencies or the changing features in our relationship to any external "Nature": we could express this by saying that we detect only that which has a time-flux. It is notable that Time has always been a major preoccupation of poets, but with a difference.

The features which we have ascribed to the scientific attitude at once confront an opposite in poetry or any of the arts; but the opposition is between ways of pursuing the aim of pattern-building out of experience which is common to science and poetry.

We found that science progresses by eliminating the personal, and reducing phenomena to ever fewer and simpler categories, whereas poetry is mainly concerned with those personal reactions which differ for every individual but recur from age to age. This may perhaps be seen in three characteristics which I have

therefore selected for illustration in well-known examples. I shall
group the first poems as suggesting how this replacement of scientific unity by aesthetic diversity leads to an interest in irresoluble
antitheses, or in situations of conflicting emotion, and therefore
to irony as a major poetic theme; the second set is grouped as
showing that certain perennial themes underlie the diversity of
ancient and modern poetic techniques; the last group shows ex-
ploitation of the notion of Time, recalling the temporal basis
that we ascribed to science. But in these poems Time has the significance of individual feeling instead of denoting the scale for
measuring external Nature.

(i) The Greek concept of *eironeia*, inadequately translated as
"irony," can express the poetic preoccupation with the opposition
between incompatibles, such as for instance fulfillment and
frustration. The following might be compared, for illustration:
Donne's "Go and catch a falling star," whose material is of the
simplest fantasy; Shakespeare's sonnet "Farewell thou art too
dear for my possessing," which employs a more complex and subtle
imagery; two modern pieces of realism, Housman's " 'Tis time,
I think, by Wenlock Town," and Dylan Thomas' "The hand
that signed the paper felled a city." None surpass in force the
extreme simplicity of expression in the Homeric lines where
Odysseus returning in disguise is recognized only by his aged dog:
"But upon the dog Argos came the blackness of death in the
moment of recognition in the twentieth year of absence." A nearly
Homeric simplicity in recent times is regained in the first and last
stanzas of Hopkins' "Felix Randal."

(ii) Scientific impermanence, the incessant supersession of
old by new, finds opposing counterpart in the perennial recurrence
of a few poetic motifs under the fluctuating technique of extremely different ages. This may be illustrated by comparing Vergil's vision of the shades pressing in frustration to cross the river
of death, with Shakespeare's King Lear awakening to half-
recognition of Cordelia, and with Wilfred Owen's "Red lips
are not so red as the stained stones kissed by the English dead."
Seldom has writing so supremely expressed the situation of des-
perate pity, and the unforgettable element in our personal response is identical over the twenty centuries.

Another poetic preoccupation, that of terror, may similarly be discovered as perennial under subtly differing techniques, by reading first Dante's approach to the infernal city of Dis, then de la Mare's dream of awakening to the death of the beloved, "Who now put dreams into thy slumbering mind?" For the very different theme of tranquillity, I suggest reading Dante's emergence into the Earthly Paradise, Spenser's *Prothalamion* with its soporific refrain, "Sweete Themmes! runne softly, till I end my Song," and de la Mare's aged shepherd, "His are the quiet steeps of dreamland, the waters of No More Pain."

All these moods have a permanence unlike the essential fluidity and progressiveness of scientific history; indeed a prototype of all that has been quoted, and in no wise inferior, might be found in the Homeric dialogue of Hector and Andromache over their child on the eve of the destruction of Troy.

(iii) I claimed that Time is the essential feature of quantitative science, but scientific time is definable in terms of scale-measure, whereas for poetry the whole concept is colored by the human reaction to opportunity and the irrevocable. There is perhaps no briefer and more devastating epitome than Housman's "Tarry delight, so seldom met, so sure to perish." The theme is familiar classically in Shakespeare's sonnets, for example those beginning, "When I do count the clock that tells the time, and see the brave day sunk in hideous night," and "When I consider every thing that grows holds in perfection but a little moment." In place of the resentment of the Elizabethan might be quoted Keats' ecstatic acceptance of Time in his first lines of "Endymion"; it is perhaps unexpected that in the present age the poetry of the acceptance of Time reappears in the last stanzas of C. Day Lewis' "Sky wide an estuary." A more contemplative vision of the significance of Time has never been better expressed than in de la Mare's "Very old are the woods." For subtle imagery, Eliot's encounter with the spirit of the dead in "Little Gidding" is as poignant as anything said by the older poets, and many readers will return also to Wilfred Owen's "Strange Meeting." Eliot's preoccupation with Time differs from that of the Elizabethan and Victorian minds in expressing, not the common resentment, but realization that Time is supreme mystery, and that to love a mystery unsolved is a step towards wisdom.

We have stressed the contrast between poetic evocation of varied individual imagery and the essential singleness of meaning in a scientific concept. This situation carries with it a contrast in technique. The imagery which crystallizes experience into a scientific concept or scientific law must be compounded out of the quantitative features accessible to all other explorers in similar experimenting; whereas for the poetic image, any fantasy will be legitimate if it proves powerful in evoking individual states of feeling, according to infinitely varied memories. Therefore what would be pernicious nonsense in law, history, or science, may be divine nonsense in poetry, and not necessarily delusive at that. Homer and Vergil are not "out of date" by clothing their immortal human sympathy in the imagery of souls which descend with the sun into the west, or of the dead who cross their dark river.

The danger at once arises that a poet may become obsessed by mere technique, and the glory of mystery degenerates into obscurity or mystification, which is abhorrent alike to science and to any art. Scientists more readily restrain one another from this danger, but their own corresponding temptation is to let the terms of their employment drown them in mere gadgetry and a forgetfulness of the aim to see Nature as comprehensive pattern.

I would suggest a study of the following poems as indicating ways by which mere technical skill develops into technique as legitimate means for arousing a state of mind. Begin from Yeats' "Byzantium," Swinburne's "Alas but though my flying song . . ." from the elegy on Baudelaire, the "Psyche," of José-María de Heredia, and the "Apparition" of Mallarmé. The subtle stage at which, without demanding explicit restriction to "meaning," a piece of verbal music develops power to convey a coherent mental imagery might be illustrated by the following poems; Shelley's "Night"; Meredith's "Lovely are the curves of the white owl sweeping," from *Love in a Valley;* de la Mare's "Sweep thy faint strings, musician"; and more recently Stephen Spender's "I think continually of those," where a finale of verbal music contributes powerfully to the vision of the past: "Born of the sun they travelled a short while towards the sun, and left the vivid air signed with their honor."

We end with a query: can legitimate technique include dissection and reassembly of a language? In many cases, this is a mere refuge of those whose command of normal usage is inadequate to their task, and recent arts are littered with such; but it is impossible to dismiss Hopkins in those terms. Three sonnets may be cited, "Carrion Comfort," "Caged Skylark," "No worst, there is none," as conveying an impression as sharply cut as any in more conventional writing. There is also the dissection and seemingly random reassembly of the poetic image itself; here it is not so easy to acquit Rilke of wanton obscurity, for example, in the third of the *Sonnets to Orpheus*, "Gesang ist Dasein. Für den Gott ein Leichtes. Wann aber sind wir?" Obscurity of image is more readily detected and arrested in scientific discipline than in the arts. Clarity of image is so great an asset as to be mentioned with honor even when the poetic content is slight; for instance, Masefield's "Cargoes."

The contrast between scientific and poetic significance of Time is one example of those disparities between the two ways of making pattern from experience which raise the insoluble query, "Does either provide insight into reality or truth?" In earlier essays, I have written about scientific and aesthetic criteria for these impossibly ambiguous words, and here there is space only to draw briefly some distinctions.

While poet and moralist, since Homeric days and earlier, have regarded clear-sightedly the fading of treasured memory and the inevitability of regret over fleeting opportunity, philosophers since Plato until nearly yesterday conceived as an urgent aim the explaining away of this, our destined slavery to Time. Some have even fallaciously invoked Einstein and relativity physics as ally. But to call in physics to redress an adverse balance in spiritual destiny has been a rash hope: we have emphasized that science is essentially a study of time-changes, but to the ultimate nature of Time it can afford no clue. Time in physics is a question of correlating quantitatively one set of events with another set which happens to define a scale. Extrapolated today to the subatomic on the one hand, and the cosmic on the other, the differential equations involving time cannot even be formally dissected without limit. In atomic physics, we find ourselves unable to adapt the large-scale perceptual treatment of time to the smallest intervals, while even the earliest and least controversial relativity enforces the fact that intervals are not uniquely dissectable into temporal and spatial. In astronomical cosmology, it has become as indeterminate to argue about the "beginning of Time," since an origin of the universe can be transformed in its equations into an infinite regress of permanent existence by altering the time-scale from the direct to the logarithmic, as de Sitter, Milne, Eddington, Dirac, and others have shown.

But two types of mind have, without any such spurious attempt to borrow from physics, sought to deny the "reality" of Time; they have thereby contended that the temporal sequence of our individual experience, and also of science's "common" experience, is some sort of illusion from which escape is possible and desirable. Firstly, there are those explicitly acknowledged to be mystics, and secondly, those metaphysicians who have chosen to assume that the universe is a multifarious manifestation of a single unity whose nature is not material.

The category of mystic must include the great Chinese visionaries of the ancient Taoist culture, also the Chinese modifiers of Buddhism, and their European counterpart, the great Catholic saints of our monastic centuries. Wisely, all these genuine mystics refrained from arguing: they simply stated that they found themselves able to train a sense of unity with Nature which liberates them from Time. Each mystic retains his inalienable right to his inner feeling, but none of them has right to claim conveyance of that state of mind to other minds. The "unreality" of Time remains for each of them secret, personal, undemonstrable but individually satisfying. The metaphysicians, on the other hand, Plato, Plotinus, Spinoza, down to Bradley and McTaggart of the present century, incorporated into their discourse a persistent claim to prove logically that Time is unreal. Such proofs are always fallacious, since they depend on uncovering self-contradictions in the concept of Time which have yielded to later discoveries in logic.

It is possible that we see in these great idealists, as in Eddington's love for the Kantian notion that Time is the mind's own imposition upon Nature, the curious fact that the acutest logical mind often contains within itself the germ of the mystical. As especially with Spinoza, the philosophy of Time's unreality is actually an expression of the mystic hidden in incongruous logical guise, and lacking only the subtlety which it might have gained from poetic imagery.

We never quite evade the feeling that some personalities are less subject than others to the dominion of Time: man lives not solely upon his sense-knowledge of an external world, and if his organization of his own internal world carries him to sufficient mental stature, he does continually create the more lasting by selecting in memory and imagination from the most transient of delights and terrors.

Now that is exactly what we found that the poet is doing.

But to estimate how lasting an individual's mental or spiritual creation will be, is certainly to dream: it is not a possibility of conscious intellect but of a faith that what we most lovingly construct is never a total loss. Many men have experienced an unprovable but ineradicable and powerful sense that there is a personal response—and perhaps a responsibility—in the universe at large, to which the decays of Nature are not the final word. This may well be the basis of genuine religion, but is wider than any single orthodoxy and will survive many theologies, and it is idle to deny that this instinct has always existed even in our uttermost disasters. But such imaginative spirit ought to claim its subtle validity without asking spurious logical support; for a disciplined imagination is not a contradiction of the logical, but complementary to it, since we showed earlier that without memory and imagination not even the simplest scientific concept could emerge from the flux of sensation.

All those mystical attitudes to Time and the universe serve to exhibit a reaction to experience radically differing from the scientific, and it is inevitable to inquire the status of poetic insight in that company. Poet, artist, and lover share something of the standpoint of the worshipper, who by his sacrifice to the "practice of an unseen presence" does actually find the material and temporal world well lost, and all four are possibly the only ones among us to realize *aeternitas* within our own time. There is no ground in science or philosophy for denying this reality of a Presence that some will call Divine, the cherishing of which is the true meaning of prayer when one can penetrate thereto through the fog of the conflicting creeds. But if the poet and the worshipper are inevitably thus mystics, they must not demand a logical as well as an imaginative or spiritual triumph over the prison of Time which we share with the animals and plants and the inanimate world.

The contention that a poetic view of Time could be akin to that of the mystics who include worshipper, lover, and idealist philosopher, will be resented in many quarters. I am, however, using the word mystic to denote not the confusion of thought more justly termed mystification, which we found abhorrent to the techniques of science and poetry alike, but to denote the acceptance of aspects of experience inexpressible in the space-time frame of science.

In fact, the one legitimate anchorage by which the situation could be judged lies in experience. When some experience, stabilized with deeply planted memories, is so strong as to overpower a man's acceptance of his fellows' valuation of the good or beautiful, his imaginative cultivation of the experience may reach a state describable only as worship; ethical and aesthetic terms are no longer adequate, and something has become sacred to him, calling forth a devotion beyond logical assessment or justification. This sense of "holiness" is as genuine to the individual as is his notion of an external "material" world, but it is not always repeatable at will and cannot readily be passed on to other people. It has thus a privacy contrasting vividly with the fact that science does not become knowledge at all until it can be communicated and its data recovered by a repetition in some colleague's measurements.

It has been supposed that because no man can share, still less dictate, the imagery of another man's most intimate experience, that therefore the religious aspect of the mystical in all of us is delusive, an idle dream of wishful thinking. Such supposition seems to me fallacious, and the fallacy is often aggravated by "rationalists" in stigmatizing the notion of the Divine as an "unnecessary hypothesis." The Divine Presence is not a hypothesis or theory for explaining things, but is a fact of direct experience by millions of individuals. We may blame the ecclesiastics who pretend that the mystical is provable as though it were logic, for this error of associating the Divine with a hypothesis. Theology, made for an age when metaphysics was an asset, not a liability, has thereby obscured the status of legitimate imagery, for instance that of the New Testament; in that imagery, both learned and unlearned can together discover that all we can know or need to know is through the symbolism of Fatherhood, Brotherhood, or Communion. These pictures, whether regarded as the religious or the poetic prerogative of the mystic in all of us, are instances of the fact that the imaginative is not necessarily the untrue or delusive. They would not gain by logical demonstration: for when we all, from time to time, exercise every man's privilege of being the child crying out in fear of the dark, the Divine answer is there for us, but is not to be held up to public exhibition. Our "belief" in it is not the mere underwriting of an unintelligible metaphysical creed, and can indeed function without the latter; belief is rather the practice of steering experience in the light of a mystic's symbols re-created in the imaginations of all of us.

On the other hand, the status of the poetic impulse may be the creation of imagery for public expression of that level of experience whose private cherishing contained the essence of worship.

I have been considering religion in a far wider sense than any tied to the churches and their conflicting creeds. So I base this meaning of worship on recognition that something important exists other than the universe of concepts constructed by scientific method out of the sense-data ordered in a space-time frame. To come to terms with this recognition is the private religion of each of us; but a man possessing not only the instincts of creative imagination but also a disciplined sense of craftsmanship will not live solely in the loneliness of individual worship of whatever he discovers sacred, but will seek expression in poetry and the arts of this deepest ecstasy of pity, terror, love, exaltation or despair.

We all respond to a poem according to the private store of memory and imaginative power, which is different in each of us; this fluctuating reinforcement would be totally irrelevant in science, but it confers upon poetry its glory of enabling today's reader to enter intimately the spiritual adventure of the long-dead writer. The struggle towards scientific truth involves the repeating of the researcher's original measurements to find under what conditions they are substantiated, but the consummation of the poet's creativeness involves the leap of the imagination in each appreciating mind in answer to the artist's original stimulus. It is to evoke this multifarious answer that the poet must become

supremely sensitive in perception and self-disciplined in technique:
he can then enshrine his experience in the exquisite word-pattern
capable of unlocking the secret places of the individual memories,
delicate, tremendous, or poignant as they severally may be.

NOTES TO CHAPTER III

1. *Confessions,* 4, 13, 20
2. Maritain, Jacques, *Art and Scholasticism* (1935), p. 3.
3. *D.D.C.,* 1.2.2
4. *Ibid.,* 1.2.2; 2.1.1
5. Exodus, 3.14
6. *Conf.* 13.32.47
7. *D.D.C.* 1.13.12
8. *Ibid.* 1.2.2
9. *Ibid.* 2.1.1
10. *Ibid.* 1.4.4-1.5.5
11. *Ibid.* 1.4.4
12. Canticles [Song of Solomon] 4.2.
13. *D.D.C.* 2.6.7
14. *Ibid.* 2.1.1
15. cf. *D.D.C.* 3.7.11 where the image is compared to the husk that
obscures the kernel of meaning.
16. *Ibid.* 12.2; 2.1.1
17. Philemon. 20
18. *D.D.C.* 1.33.37
19. *Ibid.* 2.6.8
20. *De Musica,* 6.29
21. *Ibid.* 6. 1.1.
22. *Conf.* 13.23.43
23. *Aug. de Gen. c. Man.* 1. 50. 21.
24. 1 Cor. 1.21 cf. *D.D.C.* 1.13.12.
25. *Conf.* 7.19.25
26. The idea of marriage is apposite here, yet to my knowledge, it is a
figure St. Augustine used far less frequently than other and related images
of union.
27. Proverbs 8.22.
28. John. 14.6.10
29. *D.D.C.* 1.34.38.
30 *Conf.* 13.23.38
31. *Ibid.* 13.23.36-37
32. *D.D.C.* 4.18.37.

IV

Ritual

1. *Concepts of Ritual*

Ritual is a difficult and complex subject for two main reasons. First, it is not one thing but many. We find religious and secular ritual, political and legal ritual, ritual connected with eating, with marriage, and so on. It is therefore doubtful if any significant statement can be made about it which does not admit of many exceptions. For the different forms of ritual are responses to different situations and serve different purposes in the life of the individual and of society. Men engage in ritual activities for different reasons. The activities arise from different impulses, are accompanied by different beliefs, and express or arouse different emotions. Each activity poses the questions—Does it owe its significance (1) to the situation to which it is the response, or (2) to the beliefs or emotions which it expresses or arouses, or (3) to its ritual form, or (4) to all three? The answers may be different in the case of different ritual activities.

Secondly, no piece of ritual is self-contained or self-explanatory. The observable behavior which we describe as ritual is only one element in a total reaction to a situation, an element which cannot be understood or even exist by itself. For man not only acts but thinks and feels, and action and thought and feeling are closely inter-related in the life of the individual. Similarly in religion, ritual observances, beliefs and dogmas and emotional attitudes are inextricably intertwined, and in the way of life of a society the different aspects, the ideas and purposes, the attitudes and activities, cannot be understood in isolation. Accordingly,

139

whether we consider ritual as an activity of an individual, as a religious phenomenon or as a factor in the life of a society, we cannot tear it from its context and consider it in abstraction without distorting its nature.

The consideration of ritual, therefore, raises fundamental psychological questions about the inter-relation of the different elements of human nature, such as the relative causal priority of emotions, beliefs and impulses to action. It raises similar questions about the inter-relation of the different factors in religion, the emotional attitudes, the ritual practices, and the beliefs and dogmas, and about the interconnection of the different aspects of the way of life of the society or group concerned.

What are the attitudes which promote the ritual activities and the beliefs which sustain these attitudes? Are the ritual acts sustained at the outset by any beliefs, or are dogmas and myths rationalizations to explain and justify behavior in which men engage independently of them? Again, what sort of situations occasion ritual activities? What are the purposes of those who engage in them? What emotions find expression in, or are aroused by the activities? What psychological and social effects do they produce? Are the situations to which ritual is the response merely the occasions of the ritual activities, while the form which the activities take are determined by other factors, such as social tensions? And so on.

There is, I think, no single or simple answer to such questions. The answers vary from one kind of ritual to another, and perhaps from one individual or one society to another, and some of the questions may not be legitimate at all because they are based on false assumptions about the causal relationships between the factors concerned. We find one anthropologist or historian of religion or writer on ritual putting forward a theory which covers certain forms or certain aspects of ritual and generalizing it as if it applied to all, and another putting forward a different theory that covers other forms or aspects. Such theories, so far as I can see, are not so much opposed or contradictory as supplementary. Each has got hold of a part of the truth but states it as if it were the whole. Thus, one theorist holds that the function of ritual is to give courage and confidence, to strengthen morale, and another that its function is to cause concern and anxiety; one that its function

is to meet certain needs of the individual, another that it is to con-
tribute to the survival of society; whereas, in fact, it may well do
both and perhaps cannot do the one without also doing the other.

The question which none of these theorists seems to ask is, Why
is there ritual at all? What is there in the human mind, what is the
psychological element, which is the source of the tendency to run
to ritual? All they seem to be concerned with is: What is the particular impulse or the particular need from which, or round
which, a specific sort of ritual arises? Yet the universality of ritual
and the diverse forms which it takes suggest that there is something in human nature to which it is congenial, some need which
it meets, some situations to which it is the natural response.

In dealing with a subject which is so complex and raises such
fundamental issues, I can touch on only a few points, and what I
have to say about them is tentative and provisional. Indeed, I
shall be largely concerned with asking questions to many of which
I shall not attempt to give an answer, for the simple reason that I
am not certain which, if any, of several answers is the correct one,
and I doubt if there is any answer which applies equally to all
forms of ritual.

I do not propose to begin with a definition of ritual, for two
reasons. First, there are so many different forms of ritual that any
definition covering them all would not give us much insight into
the nature of any, or indicate everything that we normally mean
by the term. This is true, for example, of the definition given in
the *Oxford Dictionary*. Ritual is there defined as (1) a prescribed order of performing religious or other devotional services,
and (2) a custom or practice of a formal kind. This is unexcep-
tionable as far as it goes, but it seems both to cover activities
which should not be regarded as ritual in the full sense and
to leave out much of what we mean by the term.

My second and more important reason for not attempting a
definition is this—Ritual seems to me to occur in more and in less
developed forms, and the concept of ritual contains ideal or normative elements which are not fully realized even in the most developed forms. And there are decadent as well as undeveloped
forms of ritual. Whether or not we apply the term ritual to the
decadent and undeveloped forms is largely a verbal question.

I might illustrate the sort of concept that ritual seems to me to be by reference to the concept of the State or of religion. In these cases, the completed concept, what the State or religion is capable of being, what we mean by the terms, can be present in a given case in a greater or a lesser degree, and perhaps it is not completely present in any actual instance. To understand such concepts, perhaps the best way is to analyze their most developed forms and consider how far others approach to these.

What, then, are the elements or factors which enter into the completed concept of ritual—that is, into ritual in the full sense as we find it, for example, in religious or magico-religious ritual? Ritual is something which we do. It has, therefore, an outward and visible form. It is, in fact, the external and therefore the social aspect of religion, or religion in action. As a form of observable outward behavior, ritual is, or involves, the repetition of precise forms of activity, gestures, words, tones, demeanors. These activities need not be elaborate or splendid; they need not involve pomp or pageantry; they may be simple and severe, but they must be formal and stylized and they must be repeated precisely and accurately.

In this respect, the tendency of the human mind towards ritual activities is one expression of its tendency to form habits. But mere routine or habit, however precisely repeated, does not constitute ritual. For the observable activities in ritual are not self-explanatory; they are symbolic. They have a meaning which is not discoverable merely by empirical observation; a meaning which the individual cannot learn for himself, as he can the purpose of ordinary practical activities. He has to be taught the meaning of ritual, be initiated into it. In that sense, ritual is conventional. The ritual activities as seen by the external observer may seem trivial or insignificant, and entirely disproportionate to the weight of significance which they convey to the initiated. Their meaning is not intrinsic, but acquired. For this reason, they are sometimes said to be routine activities which do not directly promote the physical well-being of the actors. But this account, while true, is apt to be misleading. In considering it, we must distinguish between the point-of-view of the actors and that of the external observer. For activities which are intended by the actors to promote their physical well-being and which, in fact, do so, may be performed in a ritual manner, and the actors may believe that the ritual manner of performing them is necessary to produce the practical results which follow.

For example, the primitive may believe that tilling the field and sowing the crops in a ritual manner may help the crops to grow, and even in the most developed and rational religion hopes and expectations and appeals for practical results are mingled with the motives of the devout performer as he takes part, for example, in a marriage ceremony, or in a service for rain or for the return of peace; so that the ritual character of the activities consists not so much in the kind of acts performed as in the manner in which they are performed. The manner gives them a significance which they would not otherwise have. Apart from it, they might produce the practical results which the agent intends, but they would not produce the psychological and social effects on him and on his fellows which even the outside observer can see.

These effects are usually referred to by anthropologists as the functions of the ritual. But however important the results of ritual may be, men do not engage in ritual activities in order to produce them. Ritual can produce these results only if the actors consciously and deliberately aim at, or intend, something else. For example, the primitive does not engage in magico-religious ritual in order that he may have courage and confidence, but in order that the rain may fall and the crops grow, and unless he believes that his ritual activities will produce these effects, they will not give him courage and confidence. But whatever be the conscious purpose of the actors in performing ritual activities, and whether or not these have any utilitarian purpose, ritual activities are the outward expression of certain attitudes of mind, especially emotional attitudes. Without these inner attitudes, the mere external observances or activities are not ritual in the full sense. That is why we find the ancient Chinese Record of the Rites beginning, "Always and in everything let there be reverence." When the external observances become mechanical and lifeless we have ritual in decay, religion at a low temperature, and ritual can no longer fulfill its functions either in the life of the individual or of society.

Ritual is an expression of the urge to express and to communicate, to give external and visible form to certain experiences and to convey them to others. Its appeal is primarily to the emotions rather than to the intellect, to the heart rather than to the head. It impresses without explaining, it produces results without giving reasons. Indeed, it tends to still the unsettling doubts of critical thought. That is one of the ways in which it gives comfort. It is also one of its dangers, the danger of being regarded as a substitute for, rather than a supplement to, the critical processes of the intellect. In the modern western world, especially among the better educated and more intellectual sections of the community, the main emphasis even in religion tends to be on beliefs, on conceptual thought and clear ideas, on what can be adequately expressed in words. It is therefore more difficult for us to appreciate the full significance of ritual in the lives of other societies, and even in the less intellectual and less reflective sections of the community in every society. Hence we are apt to underestimate the importance in human life of the non-rational elements and their expression. But man is not merely an intelligence; and the practical and emotional aspects of life which find expression in ritual activities must be allowed to play their part. In a well-integrated personality and a well-ordered society, each side of human nature has to be developed and given scope for free exercise. The difficulty is to maintain a proper balance between them; for while the non-rational experiences are needed to supplement the activities of the critical intellect, the emotions and the ritual activities in which they find expression need the continuous criticism of rational thought to keep them within proper bounds.

Why, then, is ritual necessary to express, to arouse, to intensify, and to communicate certain experiences? Why do we need forms of expression and communication other than verbal? There are certain psychological attitudes which cannot be directly evoked or communicated. Take emotion, for example. I cannot directly communicate my emotion to another person. I can show, say, my respect for him, only indirectly, by behaving in an appropriate manner. If I want to share my feelings with another, the best way is to engage with him in the sort of activities which are most likely to produce such feelings. Nothing is more conducive to arousing a feeling in a person than to see its appropriate expression in another. I cannot directly, by mere willing or by any other direct means, evoke even in myself a feeling which is not there. If I want to evoke such a feeling, the procedure which is most likely to be successful is to put myself in a certain situation or to behave in certain ways. Moreover, feeling is evanescent and cannot be directly recalled, or it may be weak and need strengthening. Thus, to evoke it in myself or another or to strengthen or to communicate feeling, practical activities, indirect means, are necessary, and in the case of certain feelings these practical activities must be of ritual kind. Why this must be so we shall consider shortly.

Meantime, I want to note that there are experiences not only of an emotional kind but also of a cognitive or quasi-cognitive kind, thoughts and beliefs and insights for which we cannot find adequate conceptual expression. We cannot express them clearly or adequately in words, and so we cannot make them clear to ourselves or communicate them directly to others. Such thoughts and experiences we can express and communicate only indirectly, by means of metaphors and symbols and myths—the materials of ritual. In the practice of ritual activities, and in living through the emotional experiences which they arouse, we seem to become aware of a profound significance which we can at best express only partially in words. This is especially true of experiences into which the sense of the supernatural enters—a sense which is not adequately conveyed by clear intellectual concepts but which nevertheless seems to be a form of apprehension.

The analysis of such experiences presents a very difficult psychological problem. We do not seem able to characterize the objects of which we seem to be aware in such experiences except in terms of the experiences, especially the emotional experiences, which they produce in us. Nevertheless, in living through the experiences and the activities which give rise to them we seem to become aware of something which is in danger of being restricted, if not destroyed, by attempts to express it in the rigid concepts of the intellect. To evoke and to communicate such experiences, we need ritual activities. Certain forms of ritual are the dramatized expression of certain beliefs and attitudes, and to take part in the ritual tends to evoke the beliefs and attitudes when these are absent and to strengthen them when they are weak. It does this without giving evidence, and at times against the available evidence. That is one of its dangers. It may prevent people from considering the evidence for the dramatized beliefs objectively, and may lead them to accept such beliefs not only when there is no evidence to support them, but also when the available evidence is against them.

But why do such experiences, whether emotional or quasi-cognitive, require for their expression and communication not only practical activities, but ritual? If the experiences themselves and the beliefs associated with them are so vague and varying, why do they require such formal, rigid, precise, unvarying activities for their expression?

There are certain characteristics of ritual which seem to make it appropriate for the expression of the experiences aroused on certain occasions, especially occasions which are regarded as important because they arouse strong emotion and fire the imagination:

(1) Ritual is impersonal. It is not the person so much as the part he plays which is regarded as important. Ritual drops out the purely private and personal. It is a social rather than an individual activity and therefore it is a great equalizer, like a military uniform. In the performance of his ritual role, therefore, a person may do things which would be deeply resented if he did them in his individual capacity.

(2) Ritual has a certain dignity, a seriousness and a solemnity. There is a considerable aesthetic element in it which satisfies a certain aspect of our nature. Why its precision and its formal nature should make it appropriate on important occasions, or as the expression of certain emotions, is difficult to say. We can no more say, for example, why certain patterns of color or combinations of sound are specially pleasing. All we seem able to say in these cases is that the stuff of which we are made seems to work better in some ways than in others. Which activities are more pleasing or comforting we have just to learn by experience, and perhaps we cannot give any other reason why this should be so. One experience or attitude finds its most adequate expression in poetry, another in clay, another in music, and still another in ritual activities, and what is expressed in one form cannot be completely translated into another. But while this may be true of the ritual form as such, it may still be the case that the content of the ritual, the actual activities in which the people who practice the ritual find comfort, are determined by factors in

their own social life, factors which may vary from one society to another. This may partly explain the fact that while we find ritual in all societies, the activities in which it consists vary from time to time and from society to society.

(3) Ritual can remain the same while the experiences, the beliefs, the attitudes and the emotions which find expression in it or to which it gives rise may vary, sometimes in kind and more often in degree of intensity, from individual to individual and from time to time in the life of the same individual. And (4), there seems to be an inevitability, a feeling of rightness about ritual, a feeling which demands precise and accurate performance.

Ritual resembles language and art in that all three are media both of expression and of communication. Perhaps all of them were at first mainly or even solely expressive, but in the course of their development language has become mainly a medium of communication and art has remained mainly expressive. Ritual performs both functions, but it has closer affinities with art than with language. But ritual tends not only to express, to arouse and to communicate emotion; at times it also restrains and controls it and directs it into certain channels. This is specially important in situations which naturally and normally arouse emotion so intense that it may be in danger of getting out of control. When, for example, a person's friend dies, or his son or daughter is being given in marriage, he is uneasy and restless. He may have a part to play, and in any case he wants to do something to relieve the tension. The socially prescribed ritual indicates the way in which it is appropriate for him to behave and to express his emotions. In the same way, the primitive, in the presence of forces which he does not understand and cannot control, such as those of birth and death, storm and drought—forces which arouse in him the sense of the supernatural and about which he feels impelled to do something—finds in ritual the answer to his need. It provides not only an outlet for his emotions but something which consoles and comforts him and gives him courage and confidence in the face of trials and difficulties. Or again, when a meal is taken among people of another class or from another country, a knowledge of the appropriate ritual puts the individual at his ease and overcomes his sense of awkwardness and enables him to express appropriately his respect for his hosts. Similar considerations apply to the con-

ventional ritual of ordinary everyday human relations, in family
and professions. It prescribes the appropriate way of expressing
respect for others; it restrains undue intrusion on their privacy
or undue coldness towards them. It tends to produce, as well as to
express, the appropriate emotional attitude towards them.

This brings to light another function which ritual fulfills. In
cases where the individual does not feel the appropriate emotions
towards others, or fails to appreciate the importance of an occasion,
the performance of the prescribed ritual may bring home to him
how he ought to feel or how important the occasion is. If he behaves as if he felt, he may come to feel. Now there is no doubt
that, in the case of some individuals and on some occasions, this
may be so, but this does not mean that we can found a general
theory on it, or that its being so is inconsistent with the theory that
the normal effect of ritual is to allay anxiety and ease tension.

For example, it is normal for parents to feel anxious before the
birth of a child, but some may not feel any anxiety, and in their case
the fact that among their people a certain ritual is prescribed for
them on such occasions may itself produce uneasiness—uneasiness that if the ritual is not accurately performed, all will not be
well with mother and child: this brings home to them the importance of the occasion and how they ought to feel about it. But
however the anxiety is produced, the effect of duly performing the
ritual practices is to allay it. And the situations to which ritual
is the response are situations which in themselves normally arouse
strong emotions. They are situations which for one reason or
another are regarded as important, generally because they are believed to affect the well-being or even the life of the individual or
his group. They are situations of tension, of crisis, or at least of
embarrassment. Such situations are very varied, depending on the
knowledge and experience of the people concerned. They may
be religious or they may be secular, and one form of ritual may
have among one people a religious, and among another a secular,
significance. This is true, for example, of the rites of marriage or
of coronation. But I suspect that there is in all ritual a mystical
element, a sense of mystery, a sort of religious thrill; and those
anthropologists may be right who believe that all ritual was in
origin religious, or magico-religious, and that other forms of ritual
are decayed forms.

It is certainly the religious forms which have had the most important effects in promoting the mental integrity of the individual and the social solidarity of the group. Nothing unites people more closely than the common experience of intense emotion, common concern for common objects, and the more intense the experience which they share in common the more closely it unites them, and no experience is so deeply moving as that in which the sense of the supernatural is present. Hence, religion has always united those who share it and separated them off from others.

Here I am skating over thin ice and trying to evade a fundamental issue which has deeply divided social anthropologists but which I have no space to discuss adequately—Does the sense of the supernatural come first and give rise to the emotional experiences which then find expression in ritual activities, or do the ritual activities come first and give rise to the emotion, and is the sense of the supernatural anything more than a name for the experiences which men have when they act collectively in a ritual way?

Today, the prevailing theory among many, if not most, social anthropologists and historians of religion is that the earliest form which religion took among mankind was that of ritual practices, and certainly there has been no religion without rites. According to this view, in the presence of certain situations which concern the vital interests of the group, situations of anxiety and crisis and tension, men reacted in certain ways and some of these ways they found satisfying. Those ways of acting which they found satisfying became habitual and hardened into ritual, and dogmas and beliefs were later put forward to explain and justify the ritual practices. According to this view, the reason why certain forms of activity have "caught on," become ritual, and got a wide currency, is that they brought comfort and eased tension. Because they gave comfort and eased tension, they were believed to bring about the effects which those who practiced them desired, and the stronger the belief in their efficacy the more comfort they gave.

According to one form of this theory, it is the emotions to which the collective performance of the ritual gives rise which are the source of the sense of the supernatural. Those who take this view believe that there are no gods, and that God is merely the symbol for society, and religious ritual the symbolic enactment of certain relations between the individual and society. But these are deep subjects. Origins are shrouded in the mists of antiquity, and perhaps no useful purpose is served by asking which of the three elements in religion—beliefs, ritual practices, and emotional attitudes—came first. What we can say is that wherever we find religion we find some measure of all three. They interact and mutually modify and support one another.

To me, the form of the theory which derives the sense of the supernatural from society and social sentiments seems to reverse the natural order of things. For men come together and co-operate in ritual activities for specific purposes and on special occasions, such as hunting game, or growing crops or protecting themselves. They do not come together merely or even mainly for performing ritual or religious practices; and social cohesion and collective sentiments of mutual goodwill seem to be the results or the fruits of ritual activities directed to other ends, rather than themselves the sources from which religious and ritual activities arise. I would, however, admit that the instrumental or practical uses of ritual are secondary to its expressive use.

In conclusion, I should like to note that while ritual has its uses, it has also its dangers. Its appeal is mainly to one side of our nature—the nonrational and especially the emotional side; and emotions are in danger of running to excess unless they are re-strained and checked by rational and reflective considerations. Though we regard the situations to which ritual is the response and the ends to which it is the means as of profound importance, our ideas regarding them and their significance are vague and in-definite, mere hints and suggestions, if even that. While it may be impossible to get very clear ideas about them, it is desirable that we should make our ideas about them as clear as possible, and that we should subject them and their ritual expression to the scrutiny of reason. Otherwise, we are in danger of being carried away into all sorts of emotional extravagances and of mistaking myths and metaphors for literal reality.

This is especially liable to happen when the emotions are col-lective, as in certain forms of political ritual. It may well be true that the creative and formative aspects of our nature are in danger of being restricted or repressed by the rigidity of clear concepts, but the danger of being carried away by feelings stimulated by vague and amorphous ideas to which we attach a profound significance is no less great. The collective emotions which are aroused when men engage together in certain forms of political or religious ritual may engender moral fervor, but they do not give light or guidance. As Whitehead puts it, "Intense emotions are evidence of some vivid experience, but they are a poor guarantee of its correct interpretation." "Thus," he continues, "the dispassionate criticism of religious beliefs is beyond all things necessary." And this is even more true of political beliefs and ritual. Life needs direction as well as drive, and neither of these will perform the functions of the other. It should, however, be added that part of the value of a well-established ritual is that it provides an opportunity for the orderly expression of strong and conflicting emotions and tends to prevent them from running riot.

I might sum up my main conclusions thus: Ritual is necessary to express experiences and attitudes which cannot be adequately expressed in any other way; to communicate emotional experiences which cannot be directly conveyed to others; to keep such experiences alive because emotions are fleeting; to awaken them when they are absent and cannot be recalled at will; to restrain them and canalize them into appropriate forms; to communicate the significance of situations which seem important, but of which the significance cannot be adequately expressed in conceptual terms; to give men spiritual support and to enable them to act appropriately in situations, such as the presence of the supernatural, which they do not understand and cannot control.

The effect of taking part together in ritual activities is to promote the mental integrity of the individual and the social harmony of the group, and to produce a spirit of mutual trust and goodwill which overflows into all the activities and to help face the hazards and hardships of life with renewed vigor and confidence. But ritual activities will produce these beneficial results only so long as those who engage in them believe in their efficacy: not their efficacy to produce these results, but their efficacy, for example, to bring strength and security and good fortune and to put people into a proper relation to the supernatural.

2. *Ritual Practice*

In the simpler English political world of W. S. Gilbert's *Iolan the*, a man was born either a liberal or conservative, which though in a wider sense still true, was never very creditable to the human capacity for splitting up to the utmost extent to which the divisional process is susceptible. At that time, however, the English imagination had not been so fully weaned from religion, and the sectarian spirit manifested more in that domain than in politics. And nothing is more remarkable than the fact that ritual has been one of the greatest of the rift-makers.

Doctrine has been successful enough in that respect, but hardly more so perhaps than ritual, at any rate in the Christian world. There is some intellectual basis for doctrinal differences, but the attitude to ritual can be and often is purely emotional. Many people seem to be born ritualists or anti-ritualists, and a genuflexion or an altar lamp has been the issue of a bitter controversy in the body of the English Church, while incense is regarded by many worthy Protestants as an indubitable mark of the Roman beast. A very strange psychological phenomenon in view of the fact that there is no religious sect without ritual, in however elementary a form, and the only distinction between the most pronounced anti- and hyper-ritualist, is one of degree. The tweedledumers will bow the head or kneel in prayer, but to make the sign of the cross is to proclaim yourself a tweedledeer, and to be outside the pale.

One of the unconsidered results of what may be described generally as the Protestant attitude to ritual, especially in the Dissenting sects, is the change of emphasis in worship. As ritual is eliminated the displacement in the service is made good by the greater importance attached to the sermon; indeed, the sermon becomes the essential element in the procedure. But the sermon is no part of worship at all; it is a lecture, an instruction, an exhortation; you listen, but you do not and can not worship at the same time. If worship is anything, it is an attempt to bring God and the worshiper into a personal relation, an attempt to open up a channel between the soul of the aspirant and the Divine to which he aspires, not to attend to the words of the preacher but to the secret words of God. You can share your listening with the other people in the church, you can share your singing, but you certainly can not share your individual approach to the Supreme, just because it is your approach and not theirs. Hence the ceremonial of the Mass, for example, is performed by the priest and his assistants alone. The worshiper need not follow it or even understand it; its object is to create conditions within the psychic and spiritual "aura" of the church, which will render it easier for the worshiper to rise out of himself to the source of the faith and hope which is his.

That is one of the purposes of ritual, and its practical banishment, save in the form of prayer, which as the parson's prayer may supplement but can not substitute the individual effort, has reduced the element of worship almost to the vanishing point. So much so that in the heyday of the "popular preacher" it is safe to say that for the crowds which followed him the voice from the pulpit effactually submerged that "voice of the silence" which is the bliss of worship. Faith in and knowledge of the unseen can be built only by meditation on the mysteries of the unseen, and a faith and knowledge at second-hand, an intellectual or emotional acceptance, sustained by the pulpit or the platform, often identical, is not likely to withstand any serious attack from outside, or a more attractive titillation from the rival talking-shops beyond the temple door. When doubt and weariness assert their presence there are no reserves to withstand them and hold the inner fortress of conviction till the insidious enemy departs. When in the world it is difficult enough to forget the world, and the very few strong souls who carry their temple with them and need no aids to help them to communion with reality can dispense with the crutches of the weaker brethren. Ritual is an aid, with values not to be lightly cast aside, until at least it is understood. Condemnation is a primrose path to the sterner alternative of unprejudiced inquiry.

Ritual is drama, and drama holds much the same relation to literature, religious and secular, and to art, that the physical body does to the subtle bodies. It brings abstractions into the concrete, the two-dimensional world into the three-dimensional. In the former world you apprehend, in the latter you see. The appeal of drama is for this reason universal, and there are no children and few, if any, adults who do not construct dramas in their imagina-

tion, even if they do not actually stage them in the flesh and
blood of physical action, in which they themselves play the major
role. Secular drama had its birth in sacred drama, to which we owe
not only much great literature, but most of the finest achievements
of the artist. It is said that architecture is the art which receives all
the other arts, combining and unifying them, design, sculpture,
and painting, to adorn the building, landscape gardening to provide the setting, and dancing and music to give content and life to
the vacancy within.

But in a deeper and more historic sense, ritual is the primary
assembly and source of the arts, for man reserved his highest
efforts in architecture for the temple, and the plan of the temple
was dictated by the ritual to be enacted there, and its embellish-
ments for the illustration of the ritual. The tyro in church architecture is aware that the chancel is the ritual stage, the soul of the
building, to which all other parts are subsidiary, and the High
Altar the soul of the soul, the center and nucleus of mystery and
worship, and that the nave was the processional approach. We
say "was," for processions, like the altar, savored too much of
superstition and the Scarlet Woman, and the nave of a Protestant
cathedral is now only an impressive architectural adjunct, without
use or meaning. In the High Church party the erstwhile altar
appears to hover between being a mere communion table and a
revived altar, and in the Dissenting chapel the uninspiring pulpit
generally takes the dominant place.

As the secular drama gradually developed out of ritual and
the player superseded the priest, the change-over from ritualism
to realism was itself gradual, as may be seen very clearly today in
the un-Westernized drama of China and Japan which is still semi-
ritualistic. The strongly stylized art of these countries shows also
their debt to ritual, of which the most striking examples are to be
found perhaps in the layout of the Japanese garden, and in the
elaborate Japanese art of flower arrangement. In fact, the difference between the East and West is—or was—the difference between the essentially ritualistic mind and the essentially realistic.
To the one mind things are symbols, to the other things are things.
It is lamentable, but not surprising, that in the clash between them
the things have it.

Ritual then is drama, but not ordinary drama, and as the essence of drama is action, ritual action must be something different from ordinary action. In what does this difference consist? The chief difference, and this alone separates ritual from its derivatives, is that the action is directed to an unseen end, and is concerned primarily not with other men or animals or things but with the inhabitants of the invisible worlds, Gods, angels, demons, elementals, etc. It may be purely symbolic, conveying spiritual or psychic truths by means of gesture, pose, and movements, or magical, evoking beings on the super-material planes, or liberating forces from those planes. Simple examples of each are bowing the head in prayer as a mark of devotion, which is symbolic, and the benediction of a priest, which is magical. The hands and especially the finger-tips are issuing points for forces arising within the subtle bodies, which can be concentrated and directed by will.

And here it is desirable to explain a fact on which not only the reality and efficacy of ceremonial magic depend, but all spiritual manifestations in the material world. It is a dark puzzle to most people as to why, if the spiritual powers are more potent than the powers for evil, and must ultimately prevail, they do not, when evil in its mightiest and most horrible shapes is seemingly overwhelming humanity, pour forth in an irresistible flood and sweep the evil away. What is God doing that He permits the Devil his conquering stride? The problem, like Omar's problem of the "knot of human fate," requires no intricate philosophy nor retreat into the mysterious "will of God" to solve. It is because a spiritual force must have a material channel if it is to do work on the material plane. The finest matter can not act directly on the grossest, any more than sunshine can flood a room when the windows are shuttered. The higher powers must have their human agents, whose bodies are the channels through which their influence is transmitted to the world of men. This is the fact behind the claim of the Roman church to an unbroken apostolic succession, behind the similar claim of schools of initiation into the occult mysteries, behind the role of the actors in a magical ceremonial, and in a wider sense, the role of all spiritually enlightened people in an ignorant, blind, and wicked world. When the human beings on earth are few, and the sub-humans many, the dominant tint of civilization will favor more of the Devil's palette than of God's.

But to return to the nature of the ritual act. It expresses and resumes a number of common actions, as rays or lines may issue from a common center. Thus the handshake, which is part of the ritual of everyday life, may signify affection, consolation, the joy of meeting, the sorrow of parting, all the giving and receiving of which friendship and goodwill are compact. Acts too which are purely decorative, whose end is beauty alone, are allied to ritual acts, if it can not be claimed that they are strictly so. What poetry is to prose, with its added weight of suggestion, its greater depth and brilliance of color, that a true ritual action is to the drama of the secular world. While it goes without saying that the form is of no value without the life, it must not be overlooked that though the form can not create the life, the mere doing of an act constantly with a particular state of mind can render the capture of that state of mind, when the conditions, outer or inner, are unfavorable, easier than would otherwise be the case. If you are far from a laughing mood, the automatic bringing into play of the visible muscles of the face will often bring on the mood. The mind is a rebellious instrument and hard to discipline. Ritual is a discipline, a means whereby that world which is "too much with us" may be shut off and the appropriate inner attitude attained. Those to whom ritual is just so much "mummery" ignore a patent fact in psychology, and because so much social ritual is only a form, and intended to be only a form, assume that ritual is magic and religion is necessarily in the same category. The forms have no meaning to them and therefore can have no meaning to anybody—a system of reasoning as silly as it is unfortunately widespread.

Let us now analyze the processes of a typical magical ritual. The first part of such a ritual is the delimitation of the "field" or sphere of operations. This may be done by drawing an invisible circle with an appropriate instrument, a wand, a sword, etc., and strengthening it by outlining figures, such as the five- or six-point star, i.e., the pentagram or hexagram, in the air. There are special ways of outlining these figures, according to whether they are invoking or banishing symbols. The circle may be marked by lights or a continuous ring of fire—the latter more particularly in the noetic circle of Black Magic—or in some other way as by drawing it in sand. Processions and circumambulations may either intensify the field or make it. The archetypes of all such circumambulations are the daily and annual journeys of the earth around the sun, or more accurately of the earth in its diurnal revolution and orbital progression in the course of the year. It is in this majestic ritual field that the solar and planetary forces are specialized before reaching the earth, and every magical ceremonial is a copy of it in miniature.

The field, being duly circumscribed and prepared, must be purified of matter unsuitable to respond to the vibrations of the higher forces to be brought into action, or definitely alien to them. This is usually accomplished by the sprinkling of water and the burning of incense in the four quarters, east, south, west, north. Not only is the incense a purifying agent, but the finely divided matter of which it is composed supplies a basis for the transmission of the subtle matters.

All is now ready for the ritual proper. In thinking of the field we can compare it on the lines of physical analogy to a magnetic or electrical field. The body of the operator, or bodies if there are more than one, corresponds to the conducting wires, and the current to the will. As the ritual proceeds a "stress" or psychic tension is created, which will create a similar stress in the bodies of those who may be present, though taking no part in the ritual itself. The stress is helped by the consecrated implements and vessels employed, which supplement the intoned or chanted words and particularly the "words of power," which are the essential element in any magical process and on which its effectiveness depends. If it is an invoking and not a mere "charging" ceremonial it will generally conclude with a banishing ritual which liberates the forces or beings invoked and neutralizes the field.

As the reader has probably no intention of adventuring personally into the difficult, and without preparation and guidance, dangerous domain of ceremonial magic, the application of the above conceptions to a typical ritual is fraught with some difficulty. Fortunately the Roman rite of the Eucharist affords all that is needed for our purpose. The Holy Communion of the Protestant Church will not serve, as it is shorn of all its magical elements. Nor has it the sublimity of the Sacrament of the Mass. Here there is a general and practically permanent "field," created by the original consecration of the building, within which is the immediate circle of operations resulting from the ritual performance itself. Every object used in the ceremony is consecrated by a charging

ceremonial and is employed for no other purpose. The Priest
or Hierophant prepares by putting on the garments of his office,
each of which has its meaning. The first, the cassock, is black in
color and signifies space before a field is made. He washes the
tips of his fingers, to signify the purification of the organs of action.
The garments over the cassock—six in all—indicate the subtle
bodies. Thus the prayer he repeats when putting on the stole—
the long strip of brocade worn over the shoulders, with its two ends
hanging in front of the alb, the white tunic reaching to the feet—
commences "Restore to me, O Lord, the robe of immortality,"
which is clearly the spiritual body. By the sprinkling of holy
water, the censing, and the chanting of various prayers in several
positions in the choir, the field is outlined and cleansed. The Priest
with his two assistants, the Deacon and Sub-Deacon, alternately
repeats verses of the ritual. These bring the vibrations of their
bodies into harmony, forming a living battery of force. A Clair-
voyant would see lines of trembling light proceeding from one to
the other, growing brighter and stronger as the ceremony proceeds. The great moment approaches. The Victim in the shapes
of bread and wine is offered up upon the altar. Over the bread is
pronounced the Word of Power, "For this is my Body," over the
wine, "For this is the Chalice of My Blood." At this moment tremendous spiritual potencies are in action. The subtle matter of the
hidden worlds is, as it were, drawn into a gyratory whirl, and
through the funnel thus formed pours down into the bread and
wine a great stream of spiritual energy, and from thence radiates
over the whole ritual field, both that evoked by the Priest and that
within the confines of the sacred building, fire from the exhaustless
fountains of the participating Hierarchies.

The Mass is a Catholic rite. But ceremonials centering on the
bread and wine are not peculiar to Christianity, are in fact as old
as religion and the mysteries. Bread has even been the symbol of
Sustenance, that which builds up and sustains the bodies, and
Blood a synonym of Life. Transubstantiation, the change which
is affirmed to occur in the bread and wine at the time of the consecration, is a real change. The outer appearance is not the real
bread and wine even before the consecration, any more than the
outer appearance of any object on the physical plane is the real
object. The outer appearances are composed of what are called

in philosophy the "accidents." They depend on the responses of the senses, which apprehend only a part of the physical world. Far more of the world is beyond the senses than is within their purview. The eye is incapable of perceiving more than one-seventh of the known spectrum, and a very slight change in its receptivity to visual vibrations would alter the whole appearance of that world, which seems so solid a manifestation of bedrock reality. On such a flimsy, accidental foundation rests the world on which so much of the attention and thought of man is directed. A shadow of a shadow, a dream within a dream. But transubstantiation is affirmed, not of the accidents but of the essences of bread and wine. The characteristic of dense matter is its resistance to change. Thought transforms itself in a flash. The play of light and shade is not more swift. The mind is ever changing, it requires an effort to hold it still. But though the inner man is perpetually changing, the body remains the same, what it was it is. Thought and mood will and do change it, but very, very slowly, a matter perhaps of years, not of the flying moment.

Why, then, because the bread and wine of eye and touch are apparently unaltered, is it difficult to understand that the sacramental bread and wine are no longer the same, even in their physical substances? With the transformation of the essences, the outer vehicles become the conveyors of forces which were not there before the sacramental change was affected by the cooperation of priest and the angelic principalities and powers. It is not an ordinary change, it is a magical change, and either magic is wholly a mumbo-jumbo, and spiritual power a myth, or transubstantiation is not a figment of speculative theological hair-splitting but more truly a fact than any of the facts we laboriously collect in the evanescent world of phenomena and the bodily senses. And if so, we do not stretch belief to the breaking point in accepting that description of one of the Fathers of the church, who tells us that at the climax of the sacrifice of the Mass, a great hierarchy of angelic beings reach up from the sanctuary, through whose ranks stream a sea of glory from the Divine Source above, making of the temple an ocean of living light, in which soul and body may bathe and be refreshed, taking back to the outer a strength, and a memory, and a peace which shall not readily fade away.

As we have taken our example of a magical ceremonial from

the Roman Church, we can not do better than draw on the same
source for an example of a symbolic one. Symbolism, of course,
permeates all ritual. Spiritual teaching can indeed be given in no
other way. Whether it is conveyed by words, by objects, by dia-
gram, by picture—these are symbols all. If they are words, their
dictionary meaning is nothing but a guide, an intellectual stepping-
stone, to a truth which transcends intellect. To the seer, all the
lower worlds are a divine heraldry, a shield on which is emblazoned
the spiritual pedigree of the lowliest and the most splendid forms
alike. The scientific mind finds satisfaction in the forms themselves, in the investigation of their infinite complexity, their har-
monies, adaptations, and beauties, a complexity which grows as
research grows, and which will never be exhausted. The mystic
finds no resting-place in the forms, no ultimate end to the accumulation of the facts concerning them; the bewildering astronomy of
suns and universes is matched by the no less bewildering astronomy
of atoms and cells, until figures become meaningless and significance is lost in multiplicity. The universe on that side is a gigantic
maze of cul-de-sacs. But forms regarded as symbols become no
longer ends in themselves but jumping-off places for a realm where
forms are gathered like threads into their "ensouling" ideas.

In a specifically magical ritual, there is power, forces are released; in a symbolic ritual the purpose is pictorial, a representation
of the unseen by the seen. Among the High Ceremonies of the
Catholic Church none is more impressive, or carries a greater
depth of meaning, than the Tenebrae, literally "Darkness." For
its full dramatic effect it must be witnessed in the solemn pomp of
the Sistine Chapel. It is performed on the eve of Good Friday.
The only lights in the building are the lights from the candles on
the altar. As each division of the psalms and the benedictus is
chanted, the candles, one by one, are extinguished until one
lighted candle remains. This is not extinguished but is concealed
behind the altar. Then, in total darkness, the Miserere—the fifty-
first psalm—is sung by the choir, perhaps the most sublime religious music ever composed. The ceremonial has its fitting conclusion in the relighting of the altar candles from the flame of the
concealed candle.

The orthodox explanation is that of the Passion and Agony of
Jesus. The gradual extinction of the lights is His growing suffering

on the cross. Others say the forsaking of Him by His disciples. The darkness is the darkness which is said to have fallen on the world at the supreme moment of His death. The Miserere is a representation of the mental agonies of the dying Savior.

If we apply this explanation to the Christ in each one of us— the God within—we shall see in it the drama of every human soul which reaches final liberation from the prison-houses of the bodies. The lights *are* the bodies. In the eclipse of the lights, we perceive the casting-off of the bodies, the breaking of the shackles of illusion, the resolute withdrawal from body after body, saying to each in turn, "I am not this." As the soul rises on the ladder of the worlds the prospects increase in brilliance and beauty, but as such is abandoned the inner darkness deepens, until at last the spiritual body itself is forsaken, black night descends, and the pilgrim stands alone and naked in the awful vacancy of space. His hands have grasped form after form, torn aside veil after veil, and as every veil is lifted the voice of illusion has whispered, "Rest here, for here at length is reality." In a supreme effort of renunciation, he has closed ear and eye to the flattering deception, and now his hands are empty and there is nothing more to grasp. Then in the darkness there is a gleam, the gleam broadens into a glory, and lo! he is one with the Self, bathed in the undying light of the Self, and sharing in the life and light of all other Selves. The curse of separateness is lifted. The last veil disappears. And from the immortal candle of the Self he can resume the bodies he has abandoned, as and when he will, the servant of the Universal Self in all the worlds.

It is one of the fixed ideas of the rationalistic school of religious interpretation that when a symbol has been explained in terms of a natural phenomenon it is finished with. The "solar myth" in particular is a master-key which opens the door of every major mystery, and when you have brought in the sun, the mystery is happily disposed of and there is no more to be said. But the physical plane interpretation is only one twist of the key, and there are many doors and many levels of meaning. The serial extinguishment of the candles in the Tenebrae can if you like be merely a dramatic method of bringing about the physical oncoming of darkness, and the darkness the basis and origin of the super-structure of imagination which marks the busy development of the child-mind.

It was said to somebody who expressed his disappointment with
Niagara that he did not measure Niagara but Niagara measured
him. We can leave it at that and content ourselves with dwelling
for a moment on the cosmic significance of Tenebrae. To the
reader familiar with the majestic Hindu conception of the birth
and death of universes the Tenebrae is an obvious presentation of
that mighty process. The lights are the worlds. As the manifested
God recedes into the unmanifested, and the outpouring tide of
being begins to ebb, so the life of the worlds and planes dies out.
The Day of His embodiment in time and space is over, the Night
descends. But concealed in the bosom of God remains the living
seed of the universe to be, and in the hidden light is the promise
of the future Day.

V

Natural Science and Faith

1. Kepler's Ingenuity

In examining the hypotheses and reasonings of those early Renaissance scientists who gave to modern science the initial thrust which has insured its healthful life ever since, one is struck with the inordinate, though not absolutely decisive, weight they allowed to instinctive judgments. The habit to which I refer, early developed by the forerunners of the modern scientific method, is the provisional adoption of an hypothesis, because every possible consequence of it is capable of experimental verification, so that the persevering application of the same method may be expected to reveal its disagreement with facts, if it does so disagree. Galileo appeals to *il lume naturale* at the most critical stages of his reasoning. Kepler, Gilbert, and Harvey—not to speak of Copernicus—substantially rely upon an inward power, not sufficient to reach the truth by itself, but yet supplying an essential factor to the influences carrying their minds to the truth.

For example, at a certain stage of Kepler's reasoning, he found that the observed longitudes of Mars, which he had long tried in vain to get fitted with an orbit, were (within the possible limits of error of the observations) such as they would be if Mars moved in an ellipse. As Kepler records in *De Motibus Stellae Martis* (*New Aetiological Astronomy or Celestial Physics together with Commentaries on the Movements of the Planet Mars*, pub. 1609) and repeats in his *Epitome of Copernican Astronomy* (pub. 1618-21), the facts were thus, in so far, a *likeness* of those of motion in an elliptic orbit. Kepler did not conclude from this that the orbit really was an ellipse; but it did incline him to the idea so

163

much as to decide him to undertake to ascertain whether virtual predictions about the latitudes and parallaxes based on this hypothesis would be verified or not. This probational adoption of the hypothesis was an abductive argument in the sense that it is the only kind of argument which starts a new idea. By the term "virtual prediction," I mean an experiential consequence deduced from the hypothesis, and selected from among possible consequences independently of whether it is known, or believed, to be true, or not; so that at the time it is selected as a test of the hypothesis, we are either ignorant of whether it will support or refute the hypothesis, or at least, do not select a test which we should not have selected if we had been so ignorant.

When Kepler had found that the elliptic orbit placed the planet Mars in the right longitudes, he proceeded to test the hypothesis in two ways. In the first place, it had always been comparatively easy to find hypotheses approximately representing the longitudes, although not to the point of accuracy of Tycho Brahe's observations. But when these hypotheses were applied to the latitudes, it had always been found that additional hypotheses, of librations, of tiltings of the orbit of a complicated kind, having little verisimilitude, were required to come near to a representation of the latitudes. Kepler undertook the calculation of the latitudes from his elliptic theory without knowing whether the calculation would agree with the observation or not; but it was found that it did so admirably. He then went back to the longitudes, and applied another test, of the success of which he could know nothing beforehand. What he had so far found was that the planet was at the time of observation always in the direction in which it ought to be.

But was it at the right distance? This could not be quite positively ascertained. But he could take two times at which Mars had been observed, and, at which according to the elliptic theory (which in this respect could hardly be in error) it was at the same point of its orbit, but at which it was certain that the earth was at widely different points in its orbit. The orbit of the earth is so nearly circular that there could be no doubt where it was at these times. These two places and the place of Mars (supposed the same at the two times) gave a triangle of which two angles and the intermediate side (the distance between the two positions of the earth) were known (the mean distance of the sun from the earth being taken as the unit of distance). From that he could calculate the distance of Mars from the sun, with no assumption except that Mars was really at the same point of his orbit, about which there could hardly be the least doubt, whether the elliptic orbit were correct or not. By trying this at times when Mars was at the two extremes of his orbit, and when he was at intermediate places, Kepler could get a test of the severest character as to whether the elliptic theory really flattened the orbit by the right amount or not.

In the cases of the few, but well situated, pairs of observations which could be found that were suitable to this test, the accord of observation and theory was all that could be desired, and clinched the argument in the mind of every thinking person. It will be observed that the argument was very different from what it would have been if Kepler had merely taken all the observations of longitude, latitude, and parallax and had constructed from them a theory that would suit them all. That might evince no more than Kepler's extraordinary ingenuity. Nor was the last test the same that it would have been if Kepler, looking over the observations, and hunting for the features of them that should suit the theory, had found this. That might only show that out of many features of observations, some suited the theory. But his course was very different. He did not select this test because it would give a favorable result; he did not know that it would do so. He selected it because it was the test which reason demanded should be applied.

The methods of reasoning of science have been studied in various ways and with results which disagree in important particulars. The followers of Laplace treat the subject from the point-of-view of the theory of probabilities. After corrections credited and due to Boole's *Laws of Thought* and contributions of others, that method yields substantially the results outlined above with regard to Kepler's method. In his *The Philosophy of the Inductive Sciences* (1840), Whewell described this method of reasoning just as it appeared to a man deeply conversant with several branches of science as only a genuine researcher can know them, and adding to that knowledge a full acquaintance with the history of science. These results, as might be expected, are of the highest value, although there are important distinctions and reasons which he overlooked. John Stuart Mill endeavored to explain this

scientific method of reasoning by means of the nominalistic metaphysics of his father. The superficial perspicuity of that kind of
metaphysics rendered his logic extremely popular with those who
think, but do not think profoundly; who know something of
science, but more from the outside than from the inside, and who
for one reason or another delight in the simplest theories
even if they fail to cover the facts.

Mill denies that there was any reasoning whatsoever involved
in Kepler's procedure. According to Whewell (*supra,* III, ch. 2, 3),
Mill says it is merely a description of the facts. He seems to imagine
that Kepler had all the places of Mars in space given to him by
Tycho's observations; and that all he did was to generalize and so
obtain a general expression for them. Even had that been all, it
would certainly have been inference. Had Mill had even this
much practical acquaintance with astronomy as to have practiced
discussions of the motions of binary stars, he would have seen
that. But to characterize Kepler's work as mere inference is to
betray total ignorance of it. Mill certainly never read the *De
Motibus Stellae Martis,* which is not easy reading. The reason it is
not easy is that it calls for the most vigorous exercise of all the
powers of reasoning from beginning to end.

What Kepler had given was a large collection of observations of
the apparent places of Mars at different times. He also knew that,
in a general way, the Ptolemaic theory agrees with the appearances, although there were various difficulties in making it fit
exactly. He was furthermore convinced that the hypothesis of
Copernicus ought to be accepted. Now this hypothesis, as Copernicus himself understood its first outline, merely modifies the
theory of Ptolemy so far as to impart to all the bodies of the
solar system one common motion, just what is required to annul the
mean motion of the sun. It would seem, therefore, at first sight,
that it ought not to affect the appearances at all. If Mill had called
the work of Copernicus mere description, he would not have been
so very far from the truth as he was. But Kepler did not understand the matter quite as Copernicus did.

Because the sun was so near the center of the system, and was
of vast size (even Kepler knew that its diameter must be at least
fifteen times that of the earth), Kepler, looking at the matter dy-
namically, thought it must have something to do with causing

the planets to move in their orbits. This retroduction, vague as it was, cost great intellectual labor, and was most important in its bearings upon all Kepler's work. Now Kepler remarked that the lines of apsides of the orbits of Mars and of the earth are not parallel; and he utilized various observations most ingeniously to infer that they probably intersected in the sun. Consequently, it must be supposed that a general description of the motion would be simpler when inferred to the sun as a fixed point of reference than when referred to any other point. Thence it followed that the proper times at which to take the observations of Mars for determining its true orbit were when it appeared just opposite the sun—the true sun—instead of when it was opposite the *mean* sun, as had been the practice. Carrying out this idea, he obtained a theory of Mars' orbit which satisfied the longitudes at all the oppositions observed by Tycho and himself, thirteen in number, to perfection. But unfortunately, it did not satisfy the latitudes at all and was totally irreconcilable with observations of Mars when far from opposition.

At each stage of his long investigation, Kepler has a theory which is approximately true, since it approximately satisfies the observations (that is, within 8', which is less than any but Tycho's observations could decisively pronounce as error), and he proceeds to modify this theory, after the most careful and judicious reflection, in such a way as to render it more rational or closer to the observed fact. Thus, having found that the center of the orbit bisects the eccentricity, he finds in this an indication of the falsity of the theory of the equant and substitutes, for this artificial device, the principle of the equable description of areas. Subsequently, finding that the planet moves faster at ninety degrees from its apsides than it ought to do, the question is whether this is owing to an error in the law of areas or to a compression of the orbit. He ingeniously proves that the latter is the case.

Thus, never modifying his theory capriciously, but always with a sound and rational motive for just the modification he makes, it follows that when he finally reaches a modification—of most striking simplicity and rationality—which exactly satisfied the observations, it stands upon a totally different logical footing from what it would if it had been struck out at random, or the reader knows not how, and had been found to satisfy the obser-

vation. Kepler shows his keen logical sense in detailing the whole
process by which he finally arrived at the true orbit. This is perhaps the greatest piece of inspired reasoning ever performed.

2. The Difficulties of Causality

The idea that causality may be at work in nature raises a series
of difficulties in the minds of most people. There is the suspicion
that it implies the existence of a "personal" activity "out there,"
independent of human actions, and that it is therefore a transference to inanimate matter of something only human beings exert
or apply, a form of anthropomorphism. While we can think of ourselves and of others as causes, can we imagine a piece of dead
matter acting as a causal agent? Again, we can see a piece of
material, a color, we can "see" an argument, a piece of logic, but
can we see a cause? How can we get to know and verify the existence of a cause? Is it not the case that all we ever see are objects in
motion or at relative rest? Do we ever really see a cause, and if
not, on what basis of evidence is it justifiable to assert that it exists?

The terms *cause, causality, causation* have themselves been
the occasion, one might almost say the cause, of endless confusion.
To discover the cause of things has been put forward as the task of
philosophy since the time of the Pre-Socratics, as if knowledge
of cause stood on a different footing from any other kind of understanding. So also with Francis Bacon when he writes: *"Vere scire
esse per causas scire."* To J. S. Mill, a knowledge of the laws of
causation meant the power of accurate prediction in every detail.
Both physically and logically, the present was involved in the past,
and the future involved in the present. To a particular event, a
particular cause; and all that was apparently required in order to
forecast the event in every detail was the necessary and invariable conditions under which the cause acts. What an excessive
oversimplification of the true situation this is may be presently
seen.

The medieval Schoolmen appeared to accept this view. Each
cause is the effect of a previous cause, they argued, and so they
found themselves ultimately driven to admit the existence of a
First Cause that stands behind, and to a certain extent beyond,

all other causes. This they identified with God—an argument that is still presented today by theologians as if it were an inescapable conclusion. The argument might have proceeded otherwise. If, instead of asserting that each cause is the effect of a previous single cause, we say it is preceded by a group of causes, then we are led to the prior existence of a whole hierarchy of causes that diverge or branch out like the twigs of a tree. Mill's view, that of the early nineteenth century, we say is an oversimplification, for it suggests that the universe in all its manifestations acts not merely as a large machine but as a mass of self-contained small ones. Our knowledge of the world is limited in time and space to a tiny compass of the world about us; our understanding of the so-called invariable conditions under which causes are presumed to operate is necessarily equally restricted. Causality, therefore, in this mechanical sense, if it is to be operative at all, must be completely valid even in the limited compass of small regions. This view, moreover, makes no allowance for the nature of causes being dependent upon the nature of the materials with which they are concerned. Are possibly some causes "passive" and others "active"? Are we always to expect causation to act quantitatively, or are there circumstances in which its action is confined to qualitative change?

The word *cause* itself has been defined in a variety of ways. Thomas Hobbes, for example, tells us that "A cause is the sum or aggregate of all such accidents both in the agents and the patients as concur in the producing of the effect propounded: all which existing together it cannot be understood but that the effect existeth with them: or that it can possibly exist if any of them be absent." Others have defined it as the object or event that immediately precedes a change, and which existing again in similar circumstances, will be always immediately followed by a similar change. Still others have pointed out the latitude that is used in the things or events to which the term cause is applied. For example, even the absence or removal of a thing may be a cause, as when we say that the absence of moisture in the Egyptian climate is the cause of the preservation of mortuary remains; the cause of a mountain elevation may be the denudation of the surrounding regions, and hence the formation of valleys, etc.

Prior to the middle of the seventeenth century, the conception of cause was essentially a combined philosophical and theological

one, and it is not until the scientific renaissance of the early Newtonian period, with its attempts at exact mathematical predictions
of natural processes, that a distinct change begins to set in. With it
came also a readjustment in the conception of determinism. In the
theological sense, causality and determinism were not necessarily
associated. Indeed, side by side with God as the First Cause stood
two doctrines: one doctrine maintained that man was the posses-
sor of free will, having a moral choice in his actions, albeit a will
that was in fact only free economically and socially when it
operated to fulfill the dictates and policies of the Church. Like
Galileo, one was free if one handed oneself over mentally and
spiritually trussed to the all-powerful Church. The other doctrine
maintained the principle of predestination in spite of the charge
that if God had predestined everything, it implied (according to
Cardinal Bellarmine, for example) that "God was the author
of sin, God really sins, God is the only sinner, there is no sin at all."
These were the dilemmas into which the contending schools
were thrusting each other in their battle of words. Beneath the
surface, however, this struggle was something much more significant than mere verbal argument. It was the form in which two war-
ring classes were contending for the hegemony of society. It was the
challenge of the rising bourgeoisie eager to inherit social power
predestined for them, a challenge rallying to its aid serf and
peasant against the feudal lord and the feudal Church.

From this background of theological philosophy disturbed by a
rapidly growing accumulation of mercantile, commercial, and astronomical data, there emerged the scientific renaissance. Johan-
nes Kepler, analyzing masses of astronomical data from a welter
of arithmetical detail, isolated the regularities of planetary motion,
only to maintain that the heavenly bodies were urged along their
courses by angels. Isaac Newton, a physicotheologist whose private
life was devoted to a close study of the dates and prophecies in
Daniel and Revelation, devoted his public life both to problems
of the mint and to the establishment of a mathematical and
mechanical framework to enable man to become his own prophet
in the world around him. It was essentially a period midway between science and mysticism. The body and soul of man were
being released from the thralldom of medieval feudalism. And so
the seventeenth century saw mechanical determinism beginning to

push its way to the front while God the First Cause was silently bowed to his new place in the background—the great geometer, engineer, clockmaker, the Ghost in the Machine, who in some remote beginning wound up the colossal machine, released the lever, and set it working. From then on, determinism became a calculable process, involving the numerical prediction of future events. These referred to mundane events, mere movements of lumps of matter. No moral issues were involved. Causality also began to move out of the theological field. It became a force in nature that guided these lumps of matter irrevocably along their predestined grooves. It was, to be sure, a non-spiritual force whose operation made things determinate. Behind it all, however, still stood God the Creator, the First Cause, the Cause of Causes, remote, austere.

With such a past history before us, it is particularly important to beware of importing into one's analysis of the problems of causality and determinism ideas and words that have no other justification than that they have held an historic place in a controversy that was not so much concerned with discovering the nature of objective processes in reality as providing a justification for religious beliefs of a past epoch, whether it was to offer a sanction for the continuation of the social supremacy of the feudal Church, or to justify the inevitability of the overthrow of the power of that Church by a new, emerging social class.

The problems of causality are difficult enough without appeals to essentially irrelevant issues. For example, are we today not generalizing too rashly from physical science? It may be justifiable to say that the deeper science penetrates in its analysis of objective nature, the clearer does it become that natural processes of that type can be fitted into the form of systematic law so that the behavior of objects and groups of objects can be predicted with varying degrees of accuracy. It may consequently be justifiable to assert that causality and determinism manifest themselves continually in the field of objective nature. The actions of individuals and of groups of individuals in society, however, can hardly be predicted in just this way. Dare we say, then, that causality and determinism are operative in the field of human affairs even if it be granted that they manifest themselves in the scientific laboratory? Here, it should be noticed, we have turned full circle. We began by querying whether we are not dragging

human characteristics into inanimate matter in our effort to interpret nature, and now we are questioning whether we are not
guilty of an undue extension of the scope of causality and determinism from this field back into that of living matter.

May it not be that causality is imported into nature by man
and that it shows itself in the laboratory simply because the scientist "causes" things to happen by the control he exercises over the
arrangement of his material? Is it possible that scientific laws are
man-made in a very real sense? Perhaps it is the case that there
are no laws in nature, but that they are simply created by man in
his effort to understand it. Perhaps they are implied in his methods
of analysis.

Finally, there is a very old difficulty: how can there possibly be
causality in nature side by side with the human conviction that
man is a free agent? Does causality not mean that every aspect of
nature is determinate, our actions, our feelings, and our inmost
thoughts? Then in what sense are we free at all? How could this
sense of freedom survive if it were not an objective fact? What
would be the meaning of this contradiction? And what, moreover,
would be the good of doing anything if it is in this way determinate? We would be merely a collection of marionettes making
clockwork gestures, but having a mechanically acquired feeling
that we were making these movements because we *wanted* to
make them; thinking and feeling erroneously that we could *if we
cared* have done quite otherwise. Apart from this, what can be
meant by the statement that our thoughts are determined? What is
this causality that can pass so easily from the field of matter to
that of mind producing its results with infallible precision?

These are a variety of the puzzles that spring up as soon as the
question of causality is raised in general form. And now we turn
to a difficulty of a different order. Surely if causality exists as an
actual objective something—shall we call it a force?—this
would imply the possibility of repetition of an effect by the
causal agent if, again and again, it is directed to operate in the
same circumstances. After all, in what other way could causality
be exposed to view? Yet nowhere and never does history repeat
itself exactly in every particular. If we admit the existence of a
causal agent at any moment, its operation, by definition, changes
the circumstances. How, then, can we call it the *same* causal

agent in the next moment? Does this indeed mean that we must not regard it as a causal agent but as a causal process at work, and if so, what is the constant background against which this process can be viewed and isolated for examination?

We are already getting into deep water, so deep in fact that we may feel ourselves induced to give up causality simply as a complicated and complicating fiction. If this is indeed the case, if the introduction of the notion of causality is no simplification but rather the contrary, what is the alternative? Have we to fall back on the admission that anything may happen at any moment, that the universe is an irrational chaos, that order and understanding are non-existent, a mere human fiction? All these queries and the difficulties they appear to expose must be set out for careful scrutiny and examination in the light that is shed upon them by the whole history of science, of our accumulated knowledge, of rational understanding, and of control over nature. If causality appears to have shown itself in the restricted field of physical science, can that help us, we must ask, to discern its further play in more extended regions of study.

3. At the Philosophical Crossroads

Today, many scientists would assert that a belief in causality as an objective quality in an objective situation is an old-fashioned belief; that modern science, particularly since the introduction of four-dimensional geometry as a mode of representing space-time so that world events can be traced as a network, has found it possible to dispense with causality. In its place they have substituted geometrical and logical necessity, thus imagining that when conclusions are deduced as logical necessities from certain assumptions, they have demonstrated also that active causal qualities have dropped out of the picture. It will of course appear to have done so if the scientist refrains from realizing the twofold nature of his activity and from reinterpreting his findings into the world of active reality.

In using time as an imaginary component of space and treating logical causality, not for the reflection it is of the active qualities of change in the mental habits of men, but as a self-constituted, independent, and disembodied mental necessity, the scientist tends to ignore the qualitative linkage between himself and the world in which he is intimately involved, and hence tends to give a changing process the appearance of a static pattern. But in dropping the materialist plot, he often finds himself foundering on the rocks of idealism.

This, however, is not the principal reason why most scientific theorists have tended to dismiss causality from the status of a factual quality. In their minds, it has been reinforced by certain other ideas. In the first place, there is a traditional disinclination to accord to laws that express the behavior of statistical irregularities rather than of individual particles anything but a fictitious standing as laws. This is a very peculiar species of conservatism, especially at the present level of understanding. Out of the Newtonian method of approach to natural change, where motion is always regarded as particle motion, and therefore where measurements and calculations were always simply methods for approximating the *true* value and speed of the "particles," arose the belief in a "true" and "isolated" value to such relative qualities as position and motion. Hence came the notion of determinism as something applicable to, and only applicable to, every particle in the universe, as a particle. It has to be a particle.

Causality was thus transformed into a *mechanical causality,* however difficult it was to see how this had detailed validity when the subject matter became that of human action. Individual scientific men thus divided into two camps: those who were wholehoggers and asserted that once we knew sufficient about the makeup of human beings, determinism of the particle type would still be found to hold sway; and those, including the great majority of scientists, who were content to ignore these issues altogether, classifying them as "philosophy" or "metaphysics," disinclined to be diverted from pursuing their voyage of discovery along the apparently simple, direct, and hence, only true path. They didn't even ask themselves whether that line was itself in any way determined by factors other than their own desires. Had they done so, they might have seen the modern scientific movement as itself conditioned and driven forward under causal agents of an interesting sociological nature.

The important point for us to realize, however, is that causality and determinism for both groups of scientists implied causality and determinism for particles only (or for larger things that could be regarded as particles). Finally, under the pressure of experimental fact, came two violent blows to this naïve position: the discovery of the quantum of action, and the behavior of electrons sometimes as if they were particles and sometimes as if they were waves. I shall examine this a little more closely in a moment.

For our purpose here, the significant feature of these new discoveries was this: it became at once clear that within the very inmost structure of matter there existed elements whose detailed movement could not individually be predicted by the "particle" methods based upon the old Newtonian approach. From "true" value of the qualities of these sub-atomic particles as the object of his inquiry, the scientist found himself compelled to pass to "probable" values. Uncertainty in prediction was translated into uncertainty in behavior of the individual particles, and so the previously accepted rigorous laws of behavior of bits of matter appeared to stand out as fictitious regularities that emerged from the fact that they were in reality simply huge collections of chaotically moving sub-atomic particles. To those who saw the choice only between a rigid particle determinism in every detail of the universe, with its mechanical causality, or a rigid particle determinism with no causality at all, there was apparently no option. Their choice was determined! They chose the latter. To them, it was either mechanical determinism at all levels or nothing but chaos at the very foundations of matter. And so the flood-gates of prescientific obscurantism and irrational mysticism were thrown wide open.

The leaders of modern scientific thought, the men who were creating the very techniques that might help to usher in a society in which man might at last use nature in a rational, reasonable way, sallied forth to tell the world in terms of a prescientific philosophy that all was vanity, that unreason was triumphant, and that unreality lay at the very basis of nature. With all the weight of their eminence in the world of science, we were assured that the world was a mere symbol of irrationalism in the mind of a mathematical Deity. For those of us with a social conscience, who hoped to see the scientific achievements of man turned to the elimination of the real and concrete miseries of poverty, unemployment, and world-wide preparation for war, it was a bitter moment; but it constituted a challenge which could not (indeed, must not, today) be ignored.

In what is called classical science, it was always tacitly assumed that the objective world could be studied without changing it. If a disturbance did arise from the actual process of measurement, it was an "error" that could be allowed for by a careful study of such errors. The view I wish to express here denies this point-blank. It denies it in the fact that we recognize the qualitative, indeed the active qualitative, relations that exist between human beings and their environment. From that older assumption, modern science has emancipated itself to some extent, but not completely. Let us trace what effects this new standpoint has had.

Two problems now emerge. One is to attempt still to give an objective picture of the universe in the large, at the grand level, in which allowance is made for the intrusion of human beings on that scale. This intrusion shows itself there simply in the partial view which each of us gets of the same large-scale universe. Earlier in our century, this was the approach associated with the name of Einstein, and with his general and special theory of relativity. Basing his analysis on the observed fact that all measurements of the speed of light, whether one is moving towards, or away from, the source or across the direction of the beam at the moment of measurement, always lead to the same result, Einstein devised a form of description (basically one of assigning tensorial functions to vectorial spaces) that would apply to any observer irrespective of his discrete and local position in space or his particular state of motion. To achieve this, however, involved a denial of any universal meaning to the words "simultaneous events." This implied simply that space and time were not separately the absolutes of classical science and in the last resort, could not be dissociated. This phenomenological fact is implicit in the view here expressed, that change is the essential, first quality we encounter and that our time and our space are merely our slices of the unity which change involves.

From the constancy of the speed of light, it follows that two observers moving with different speeds will see successive events differently spaced, although their succession will not be altered; each will have his "slice" of space and time. This has no practical significance for individuals like ourselves on the same earth:

its importance, however, rests on the fact that it forces scientific description on the grand scale into a new logical framework. From this view, Einstein followed out the geometrical necessities of his space-time world, as a static four-dimensional world picture, and concluded that it must exhibit a behavior in the movement of bodies identical with that exhibited by gravitation. What would have ordinarily been regarded as a causal quality in the past became a geometrical necessity. The experimental basis for this standpoint is, of course, very slight, but that need not detain us. Nor need the later generalizations that succeeded in unifying a series of other large-scale phenomena into a coherent and logically satisfactory system. What is important for us to realize is that here is an isolate of the universe on such a scale that the part played in it by human action fades into the background and manifests itself only in this: that the picture is actually drawn by human beings. Even that aspect is then itself reduced to the extent that the final outline is one that is relevant to every human being. Each individual can find his picture in the general scheme if the angle from which he is viewing it can be stated.

The second type of isolate must then be very much nearer ourselves. It must treat of the way in which human beings are related to the changes that take place in the rest of the universe. It would concern itself with the interaction between man and his environment. For the scientific man nurtured in the old tradition that imagined everything could be studied without interference, this is by far the most puzzling field, for it includes the whole of social and individual activity. Within this field falls science itself. The procedure that is usually adopted follows a plan which guides each experiment in such a way as to isolate the process under consideration from the effects of extraneous disturbances, including, of course, the experimenter. This is according to the old tradition; that, however, was only the attempted method. In practice, after a certain stage of detail had been reached, it failed, as we would perhaps expect it to fail, because of the necessary qualitative relation between the experimenter, including his measuring apparatus, and the process measured. I shall attempt, in a brief example, to describe how this occurred and to examine the nature of the reaction it produced among scientific men. That reaction will best be seen not alone in their astonishment, but in the type of rationalizations they found themselves compelled to adopt to explain this unprecedented experience.

The trouble may be said to have begun with the nature of light. Until less than seventy years ago, light was firmly believed to be a pure wave-motion, the evidence for which rested on an elaborate series of experiments. These showed that it was possible to produce "interference patterns," as they are called, an effect characteristic of all other wave-motions, such as the criss-cross pattern seen on the surface of a pond when two sets of waves pass one over the other. From the standpoint of this essay, a train of waves is considered a statistical phenomenon, of which each wave in itself would be the atomic element. The wave could also be a statistical isolate of which each moving particle that assisted in forming the shape, as a totality of particles, was again an atomic isolate. A train of waves passing over the surface of the pond, for example, would appear statistically as a continuous process, for as the waves reached the shore and broke, they would appear to have done so discontinuously. In such a system, therefore, one might indeed expect to discover both continuous and discontinuous effects if observed and measured at different levels.

Two hypotheses developed in the early years of the twentieth century confused the question even more. In 1900, Max Planck pointed to the existence of discontinuous increments in energy in the heat radiated from a hot body; and later, in 1905, Einstein showed that the electrified particles that were emitted from a sensitive plate when a beam of light fell upon it implied that light had a corpuscular constitution made up of photons.

To subsequent physicists, the idea that a shower of particles could also at the same time be regarded as a train of waves came as a shock. Suddenly called upon, as they were, to reconcile two totally diverse conceptions in one and the same physical entity, the conception of a particle with a specific velocity, moving in space in a definite way, and the conception of a continuous wave extended throughout a region of space, they accepted the strange view with considerable misgivings. Planck's Law, an attempt to harmonize both concepts by linking up the measures of the two types of isolate, connected the two modes of description by stating that the kinetic energy of the particles was a definite number of times (Planck's constant) the number of vibrations per second of the wave. While Bohr pointed out that this principle of Planck's introduced an irrational feature into the description of nature, it was not contended that nature itself was in any sense irrational in its behavior. The inconsistency, it was asserted, existed solely in the mode of description.

A further measure, in this connection, was later introduced by physicists to link up the two processes, but it did so by introducing probability, which manifestly ought to have been introduced from the beginning when dealing with a statistical isolate. It stated that the intensity of the wave in any small region of the shower of corpuscles was proportional to the probability that a particle might be present in that region. The shower of photons at one level, as a stream, produces the effect of the wave system; at another level, it is a stream of particles whose appropriate measure is a probability—namely, the probability that through a given region of space at any given moment, a particle will be found to be passing.

Now it is important to note that I am not here referring to any particular photon. Virtually nothing is known about the special behavior of individual photons except of course that they exist in the stream and that they do behave. As I have already implied earlier, one must exercise great caution in discussing the appropriate measure as a probability, especially when one does not ask, nor endeavors to answer, any illegitimate question. No one has knowledge that enables him to say where exactly a particular photon will be; nor does one even know how one photon differs from another. The very conception of a photon is a statistical one, and therefore the measure of probability must be used with great circumspection if it is to be interpreted in individual terms.

Finally, in this rather involved sequence of discoveries, we come to the last law, the so-called Uncertainty Principle of Heisenberg. This examines the possibility of finding sufficient data to enable a prediction to be made of the motion, energy level, and track, of an individual photon. If the usual deterministic method is to be applied to a photon as a particle, it is necessary to state as accurately as possible both the position and the speed (in this case actually the momentum) of the photon at a given, particular moment, and these must be specified independently. Without this, one cannot expect on Newtonian principles to trace out its future track. It turns out that this cannot be done, even in theory. For Heisenberg's argument shows that the more closely we try to localize the position of the photon, by reducing the region within which it is to be observed, the more widely divergent are the possible velocities of the photons that may be found to pass through this small space. Roughly, it may be seen in this way:

At a particular point of the wave system, the intensity, and therefore the probability, of the occurrence of a photon is fixed. If we try to limit the region within which it has to be found, it would become less likely that a photon with a narrow limit of velocity will be located. If we are obliged, therefore, to keep the probability fixed, we must allow a greater latitude in the range of velocity that is admissible for our photon. If, in other words, the latitude in fixing position is decreased, the latitude in fixing velocity must be proportionally increased.

This to be sure, is only a rough and ready method of looking at it, but it brings out the point that localization in space and delimitation of velocity for a particular element of a statistical isolate are mutually inconsistent processes. But quite apart from this, it is easily shown that even if we were to attempt to examine the detailed behavior of such an elementary particle through, say a microscope, it would not be possible. The smallest quantum of light-energy that would make an electron visible, for example, would also give it such a blow as to disturb it both in position and in momentum. Moreover, the energy to see it would profoundly affect the actual features we proposed to examine. Here, then, at the very fringes of experimental practice in particle physics, the physicist is faced with a basic reason why he cannot hope to exclude himself from influencing the course of the experiment, no matter how carefully he performs the task.

I have gone into these matters at such length, not because of the intrinsic theoretical importance of this particular field, which is great, but because from the standpoint of causality and determinism, the reaction of scientists to these matters has been of such interest. I should perhaps at this point explicitly state my position on this problem as it would appear from the standpoint adopted in the early part of this essay.

In the first place, there is no intrinsic contradiction involved in the fact that the same large-scale statistical isolate may act as a statistical isolate of a wave-like nature with reference to one of its group qualities, while with reference to other group qualities it behaves as a stream of particles. Even an avalanche of stones can behave like that if it comes down in surges. One might go even further and invert the picture, as in the commonplace illustration I have given of the waves breaking on a shore, where each breaking wave can certainly be regarded as an atomic isolate so that the succession of blows acts like a stream of individual impacts.

In the second place, the specification of a statistical isolate is naturally expressible, as we have seen, in terms of probability, and when interpreted in terms of the atomic elements, implies nothing more than the appropriate type of prediction of what is to be found at a particular region of that isolate. There is no intrinsic uncertainty, in that sense, about the actual behavior. Although it cannot be isolated in an absolutely concrete way, the particle does have a unique behavior if it is a unique particle. Moreover, and most significantly the fact that it is not physically possible to obtain the data required to carry through the necessary prediction for an isolated electron or a photon asserts that mechanical determinism cannot be applied at that level.

For this reason, in addition, it also requires a different level of causality. The fact that the appropriate measurements are probabilities is itself evidence of this, but unfortunately scientists have not yet come to see that such measures do indicate the existence of causality. To them, causality is always mechanical causality, at the level of Newtonian dynamics. Accordingly, when faced with these difficulties, they have seen no choice except that between universal mechanical causality and no causality at all. Taking a rigorous mechanical view of the situation, they have almost unanimously chosen to assert that causality has disappeared *in toto* from the scheme of science, because in this case mechanical determinism was seen to be inapplicable. With the recognition of levels and their appropriate measures, the path, they doubtless believed, would be cleared for a deeper logical and philosophical development.

The surprise with which twentieth-century scientists have greeted the discovery that the very experimental conditions required to view a moving electron are themselves conditions incompatible for the electron to be viewed undisturbed must be taken as an indication of the strength of the tradition that all scientific work can be carried through in such a way as to switch the experimenter out of the picture. Here in this remote but growing point of physical science, he has belatedly discovered in the twentieth century what would be apparent to him if only he looked through the window of his laboratory at the world outside. The remarkable feature of their work on which scientists are entitled to pride themselves is their skill in discovering so many aspects of nature that can be handled in this isolated way under controlled conditions; that is, so many situations where the factor of human interaction is reduced to negligible proportions.

Finally, in this connection, and in summary, let us recall the two types of isolate of a very general nature to which attention was originally directed at the beginning of this essay. First, they were those on a grand or cosmic scale (with which Relativity theory has concerned itself) in which the affairs of men did not directly enter except through the mode of description. Second, they were those that were explicitly concerned with the interactions of man with his environment, social affairs, problems of human society, of which science and experimental investigation are but one detail. It will be acknowledged that in the pursuit of studies in this latter field, scientists have, as far as it has been possible, carried forward the traditional method learned in the first field. But in doing so, they have naturally found themselves compelled to confine their attention to a restricted set of social problems. To be sure, there have been other reasons of a social nature that have contributed towards this segregation of scientific interests. To me, however, the significant point is that in driving this method through to its experimental and logical limit, they have finally found themselves faced with a study of the very kind of interaction their methodology has been designed to avoid. Indeed, we are witnessing the long-awaited transformation of the qualitative relation of scientific method to the material it has to analyze.

VI

Secularism and Ethics

1. *After Secularism—What?*

In most Jewish circles today, it is a commonplace that if it is possible to speak of God, it is only because God has spoken of himself. We have knowledge of him, the argument runs, through the instrument of our biblical or "natural religion," which expresses God's revelatory word through nature in what we have become accustomed to term a pure state, i.e., not as mere elaborations or as attributes. Furthermore, it is said that we believe that we have knowledge of God as he manifests himself to man in progressive stages of creation and unfolding—through his image, which we call his spirit, and through his prophets. Yet despite our occasional syncretist sense that our religious faith of Judaism is a mere phase in the history of religions, an incomplete and even perhaps inadequate experience of God which only partially witnesses a single and idiosyncratic form of the "transcendental unity" of all religion, it is good from time to time to take comfort from the thought that our faith is not merely a manifestation of an immanent evolution of the religious genius of mankind, of which *my* particular faith may simply be a relatively higher expression; for if religious faith manifests anything at all, it is the fact of the intervention in human history of a transcendent God who introduces all of us into a domain which is radically closed to man in general. But it must be confessed that our religion, and our commitment to a certain quality of life that acknowledges a source beyond itself, is not the same thing at all as the idea that this source, or this "Other," is unfolding to us that which otherwise would be hidden,

183

whether or not we choose to attribute to this source predicatives, attributes, or traits of the Divine. Indeed, in this sense, the faith of the Jewish religion may be justifiably opposed to revelation.

Today, when it is so common to hear so many fundamental questions raised, which within the milieu of both our religion and our encompassing society provoke lively debate and even deep division—questions such as "Yet God is silent?" or "Are not the horizons of our religion shrouded in impenetrable gloom?"—the genuine secularists are recognizable by their having moved far beyond what they believe to be merely "dialogist" questions asked by religious men of other religions; the Jewish secularists contend that the very posing of such questions obliges the questioner to stand in some sort of proprioceptive and balanced relationship with the beliefs of all religions. Indeed, they assert that the asking of such questions is the inevitable consequence of vain endeavors on the part of men of religious faith to bring the beliefs of religion into more or less agreeable harmony with various modern conceptions of the natural world. In short, they argue that to ponder these imponderables is to become an apologist for religion, which, in their sense of the term, includes all those who are still within the field of force or sphere of influence of any sort of belief in transcendent and supra-sensory realities, whether the belief be traditionally biblical, idealistic, anthroposophical, communitive, or mystical in form.

Our Jewish secularists, then, demand that men of faith treat them with unusual consideration, because they are, apart from matters of belief, men exemplary in all things. It is, moreover, characteristic of the genuine secularist that events in the world do not seem in the least obscure or problematic to him, but perfectly clear and intelligible. He is not only serene but silent; accusations against divine order or revelation are no longer uttered at all. With the collapse of what he feels to be naïve, providential concepts of order, all complaints against the ordering of the world and all questions concerning the reasons for it have lost all their meaning for him; and, unlike the circus hand who drugs his lions before entering the cage, the Jewish secularist in our midst chooses to hunt what he understands to be the wild beast of concrete, social reality in the jungle where it lives.

In short, the secularist proposition that the study of the "social realities" of religion is the key to understanding the relationship of man to society is a concept gaining more credibility, for if religion, as they argue, is defined in functional terms, then religion is perhaps the most significant of those compound systems of meaning and expression that permit man to transcend his own limits. Today, individuals like Crusoe, who have been accustomed to function in isolation around separate and autonomous poles of subjective processes and precarious private systems, have increasingly come to feel that they can assure "self-hood" only by traversing a communal path whose end is the construction of an objective, moral universe of meaning. Indeed, it has become virtually a commonplace in contemporary Jewish America that it has been by this means—a process of building the self and society in relation to shared worldviews—that sacred meaning is revealed to man.

Though they assert that this process has been historically normative in Western religions, it should be acknowledged that the resultant symbol systems and their corresponding structural embodiments have taken many forms and varied widely: institutional denominationalism, religious organizations, particular texts, doctrines, rituals, and so on. In our contemporary Jewish milieu, therefore, when such official models have visibly deteriorated, or more properly, seem to have been frozen into immobile forms so that they can no longer cope either with a literate, mobile society under rapidly changing conditions or with the contextually religious problems and issues of selfhood and society, religion and religiosity have indeed appeared in novel, disguised, and often unexpected forms. But if modern man has indeed generated new religious beliefs and structures, it must be recognized that these new forms are often invisible because most of us have been trained and conditioned to perceive (and respond to) traditional forms.

Since Richard Niebuhr, Martin Buber, and Franz Rosenzweig, it has become customary to speak of the personal and social sources of denominationalism; but now, the Jewish secularist is making it not only possible, but necessary, for the rest of Judaism to speak of the social sources of non-denominationalism as well, i.e. the explicit and intense relationship that has developed between the increasing socialization of modern man and the decreasing in-

ternalization by the modern Jew of the traditionally sacred models
of his society. Simply to recognize the increasing secularization
of modern American Jewry is not enough, for the problems of
ultimate meaning remain.

But ultimate meanings notwithstanding, this much may be
observed about "non-denominationalism" in this specialized, social world of contemporary Jewish America that is fundamentally
different from anything our faith has experienced before: as-
sortments and groupings of heterodox ideas and concepts have
been fashioned by our clergy, laymen, and intellectual spokesmen
alike into precarious subjective systems which herald ultimate
significance. As subjectively oriented social systems, each with
its functional and autonomous rationality, each tends to reinforce
man's sense of isolation from his milieu and each interacts with
the new (commonly held) Sacred idea—the absolute autonomy of
the individual. Furthermore, the new religious forms are characterized by a nearly total absence of traditional obligations of
faith, i.e. belief in the divinity of either God or the natural world
is gratuitous and entirely voluntary; but while the new forms support, hasten, and radicalize the depersonalization of society, they
also "sanctify" by ritual fictions and acts the liberation of man's
consciousness from the strictures and constraints of the social
structure. Before any final judgments are made of the long-range
effects on Judaism of these new forms, it would perhaps be well to
examine with more care the effects upon the individual Jew; to
"depersonalize" the Jew in twentieth-century America may result
in a condition of virtually absolute human freedom; and then
again, it may once again cast him into another wilderness, and
leave him to wander without compass, adrift in the desert alone
and abandoned. For the committed Jew, today, as it has always
been with his ancestors, only time will tell.

2. *Is Anything of Vital Importance?*

By those who have no powers of observation to see what sort
of men conservatives are, true conservatism, which is senti-
mental conservatism, is often called stupid conservatism, an
epithet far more applicable to the false conservatism that looks

to see on which side bread is buttered—true conservatism, I say, means not trusting to reasonings about questions of vital importance but rather to hereditary instincts and traditional sentiments. Place before the conservative arguments to which he can find no adequate reply and which go, let us say, to demonstrate that wisdom and virtue call upon him to offer to marry his own sister, and though he be unable to answer the arguments, he will not act upon their conclusion, because he believes that tradition and the feelings that tradition and custom have developed in him are safer guides that his own feeble ratiocination. Thus, true conservatism is sentimentalism. Of course, sentiment lays no claim to infallibility, in the sense of *theoretical* infallibility, a phrase that logical analysis proves to be a mere jingle of words with a jangle of contradictory meanings. The conservative need not forget that he might have been born a Brahmin with a traditional sentiment in favor of *suttee*—a reflection that often tempts him to become a radical. But still, on the whole, he thinks his wisest plan is to reverence his deepest sentiments as his highest and ultimate authority, which is regarding them as (for him) practically infallible—that is to say, infallible in the only sense of the word in which infallible has any consistent meaning.

The opinion prevalent among radicals that conservatives and sentimentalists generally are fools is only a cropping-out of the tendency of men to conceited exaggeration of their reasoning powers. Uncompromising radical though I be upon some questions, inhabiting all my life an atmosphere of two parts art and one part science, and not reckoned as particularly credulous, I must confess that the conservative sentimentalism I have defined recommends itself to my mind as eminently sane and wholesome. Commendable as it undoubtedly is to reason out matters of detail, yet to allow mere reasonings and reason's self-conceit to overslough the normal and manly sentimentalism which ought to lie at the cornerstone of all our conduct seems to me to be foolish and despicable.

Philosophy, after all is, at its highest evaluation, nothing more than a branch of science, and as such is not a matter of vital importance; and those who represent it as being so are simply offering us a stone when we ask for bread. Mind, I do not deny that a philosophical or other scientific error may be fraught with disastrous consequences for all of mankind. It might conceivably even bring about the extirpation of the entire human race. Importance in that sense it might have in any degree. Nevertheless, in no case is it of vital importance.

A great calamity the error might be, *qua* event, in the sense in which an earthquake, or the impact of a comet, or the extinction of the sun would be an important event, and consequently, if it happens to lie in the line of my duty or of yours to investigate any philosophical question and to publish the more or less erroneous results of our investigations; I hope we shall not fail to do so, if we can. Certainly, any task which lies before us to be done has its importance. But there our responsibility ends. Nor is it the philosophy itself, *qua* cognition, that is vital, so much as it is our playing the part that is allotted to us.

You will observe that I have not said a single word in disparagement of the philosophy of religion, in general, which seems to me a most interesting study, and at any rate, possibly likely to lead to some useful result. Nor have I attacked any sect of that philosophy. It is not the *philosophy* which I hold to be baleful, but the *representing it to be of vital importance*, as if any genuine religion could come from the head instead of from the heart.

Somewhat allied to the philosophy of religion is the science of ethics. Is is equally useless. Now books of casuistry, indeed, using the word "casuistry" not in any technical sense, but merely to signify discussions of what ought to be done in various difficult situations, might be made at once extremely entertaining and positively useful. But casuistry is just what the ordinary treatises upon ethics do not touch, at least not seriously. They chiefly occupy themselves with reasoning out the basis of morality and other questions secondary to that. Now what's the *use* of prying into the philosophical basis of morality? We all know what morality is: it is behaving as you were brought up to behave, that is, to think you ought to be punished for not behaving. But to believe in thinking as you have been brought up to think defines conservatism. It needs no reasoning to perceive that morality is conservatism. But conservatism again means, as you will surely agree, not trusting to one's reasoning powers. To be a moral man is to obey the traditional beliefs and maxims of your community without hesitation or discussion. Hence, ethics, which is reasoning out an explanation of morality, is—I will not say immoral, for that would be going too far—composed of the very substance of immorality. If you ever happen to be thrown in with an unprofessional thief, the only very bad kind of thief, so as to be able to study his psychological peculiarities, you will find that two things characterize him; first, an even more immense conceit in his own reasoning powers than is common, and second, a disposition to reason about the basis of morals.

Ethics, then, even if not a positively dangerous study, as it sometimes proves, is as useless a science as can be conceived. But it must be said, in favor of ethical writers, that they are commonly free from the nauseating custom of boasting about the utility of their science.

But far be it from me to condemn. Though I was raised in New York, I shall hardly be mistaken for a Wall Street Philistine. A useless inquiry, provided it is a systematic one, is pretty much the same thing as a scientific inquiry. Or at any rate, if a scientific inquiry becomes by a mischance useful, that aspect of it has to be kept sedulously out of sight during the investigation or else its hopes of success are fatally cursed.

As long as ethics is recognized as not being a matter of vital importance or in any way touching a man's conscience, it is, to a normal and healthy mind, a civilizing and valuable study— somewhat more so than the theory of whist, much more so than the question of the landing of Columbus, which things are insignificant not at all because they are useless, nor even because they are little in themselves, but simply and solely because they are detached from the great continuum of ideas.

It would be useless to enumerate the other sciences, since it would only be to reiterate the same declaration. As long as they are not looked at as practical, and so degraded to pot-boiling arts —as today's modern writers on religion degrade the philosophy of religion, in claiming that it is practical for it is secular—for what difference does it make whether the pot to be boiled is today's or the hereafter's? They are all such that it would be far too little to say they are valuable to us. Rather let our hearts murmur "blessed are we" if the immolation of our being can weld together the smallest part of the great cosmos of ideas to which the sciences belong.

Even if a science be useful—like engineering or surgery—yet if it is useful only in an insignificant degree as those sciences are, it still has a divine spark in which its petty practicality must be forgotten and forgiven. But as soon as a proposition becomes vitally important—then in the first place it is sunk to the condition of a mere utensil; and in the second place, it ceases altogether to be scientific, because concerning matters of vital importance, reasoning is at once an impertinence toward its subject matter and a treason against itself.

Were I willing, that is to say, were I in a position I do not happen to be in, to make a single exception to the principle I am here enunciating, and to admit that there was one study which was at once scientific and yet vitally important, I should make that exception in favor of logic; for the reason that if we fall into the error of believing that vitally important questions are to be decided by reasoning, the only hope of salvation lies in formal logic, which demonstrates in the clearest manner that reasoning itself testifies to its own ultimate subordination to sentiment. It is like a Pope who should declare *ex cathedra* and call upon all the faithful to implicitly believe on pain of damnation by the power of the keys that he was *not* the supreme authority.

Among vitally important truths, there is one which I deeply believe—and which men of infinitely deeper insight than mine have believed—to be solely important. It is that vitally important facts are of all truths the veriest trifles. For the only vitally important matter is *my* concern, business, and duty—or *yours*. Now you and I—what are we? Mere cells of the social organism. Our deepest sentiment pronounces the verdict of our own insignificance. Psychological analysis reveals that there is nothing which distinguishes my personal identity except my faults and my limitations—or if you please, my blind will, which it is my highest endeavor to annihilate. Not in the contemplation of "topics or themes of highest or most vital importance" but in those universal things with which philosophy deals, the factors of the universe, is man to find his highest occupation. To pursue topics of vital importance as the first and best can lead only to one or another of two determinations —either on the one hand what is called, not unjustly, Americanism, the worship of business, the life in which the fertilizing stream of genial sentiment dries up or shrinks to a rill of comic tid-bits, or else, on the other hand, to monasticism, sleepwalking in this world with no eye nor heart except for the other. Take for the lantern of your footsteps the cold light of reason and regard your business, your duty, as the highest thing, and you can only rest in one of those goals or the other. But suppose you embrace, on the contrary, a conservative sentimentalism, modestly rate your own reasoning powers at the very mediocre price they would fetch if put up at auction, and then what do you come to? Why, then, the very first command that is laid upon you, your quite highest business, and duty, becomes, as everybody knows, to recognize a higher business than your business, not merely an avocation after the daily task of your vocation is performed, but a generalized conception of duty which completes your personality by melting it into the neighboring parts of the universal cosmos. If this sounds unintelligible, just take for comparison the first good mother of a family that meets your eye, and ask whether she is not a sentimentalist, whether you would wish her to be otherwise, and lastly, whether you can find a better formula in which to outline the universal features of her portrait than that I have just given. I dare say you can improve upon it; but you will doubtless find one element of it is correct—especially if your understanding is aided by the logic of relatives—and that is that the supreme commandment of our western religions is, to generalize, to complete the whole system even until continuity results and the distinct individuals weld together. Thus it is, that while reasoning and the sciences of reasoning strenuously proclaim the subordination of reasoning to sentiment, the very supreme commandment of sentiment is that man should generalize, or what the logic of relatives shows to be the same thing, should become welded into the universal continuum, which is what truly objective reasoning consists in. But this does not reinstate reasoning, for this generalization should come about, not merely in man's cognitions, which are but the superficial film of his being, but objectively in the deepest emotional springs of his life. In fulfilling this command, man prepares himself for transmutation into a new form of life, the joyful Nirvana in which the discontinuities of his will shall have all but disappeared.

Do you know what it was that was at the root of the barbarism of the Plantagenet period and paralyzed the awakening of science from the days of Roger Bacon to those of Francis Bacon? We plainly trace it in the history, the writings, the monuments, of that age. It was the exaggerated interest men took in matters of vital importance.

Do you know what it is in Christianity and Judaism that when recognized makes those religions agents of reform and progress? It is their marking duty as their proper finite figures. Not that it diminishes in any degree, their vital importance, but that behind the outline of those huge mountains it enables us to descry a silvery peak rising into the calm air of eternity.

WITHDRAWN

The King's College Library
New York, NY
www.tkc.edu

WITHDRAWN

108062

BL 50 .P55
Plotkin, Frederick.
Faith and reason

THE KING'S COLLEGE LIBRARY
BRIARCLIFF MANOR, N.Y. 10510